D1580886

100 WINNING BRIDGE TIPS
new edition

Learning from bitter experience at the bridge table is a slow, painful and often costly business. Most of us would turn grey on the head and long in the tooth before absorbing enough knowledge to play a competent game of bridge if we rely on nothing more than experience.

There is no need to despair, for help is at hand. This book by the well-known author, Ron Klinger, is written for improving players with the express aim of cutting down on the agony and speeding up on the process of learning. The 100 winning tips cover specific situations in bidding, play and defence, the sort of problems that arise over and over again in everyday play. Thus they provide a painless substitute for experience.

The idea is to learn how to avoid the many pitfalls and how to deal with the common problems in advance so that they will not appear unfamiliar and daunting when you meet them at the bridge table. You do not need to fall where others have fallen before you. Those who apply themselves seriously to this book can expect their game to be lifted to a much higher level. Isn't that your wish?

The original edition of this outstandingly successful book was reprinted no fewer than eight times. In this new edition the original tips have been revised, new ones added and it includes some fresh illustrative deals.

Ron Klinger is a leading international bridge teacher and has represented Australia in world championships since 1976. He has written over forty books, some of which have been translated into Bulgarian, Chinese, Danish, French, Hebrew and Icelandic.

100 WINNING BRIDGE TIPS

new edition

Ron Klinger

CASSELL
IN ASSOCIATION WITH
PETER CRAWLEY

First published in Great Britain 1987
in association with Peter Crawley
by Victor Gollancz Ltd
Eighth impression 2000

This new edition first published 2003
Third impression 2004
in association with Peter Crawley
by Cassell
Wellington House, 125 Strand, London WC2R 0BB
an imprint of the Orion Publishing Group

A catalogue record for this book
is available from the British Library

ISBN 0 304 36587 4

Typeset by Modern Bridge Publications
P.O. Box 140, Northbridge NSW 1560, Australia

Printed in Great Britain by
Clays Ltd, St Ives plc

Contents

TIPS 1-10: The Rule of 1 to the Rule of 10

TIP 1:

The Rule of 1: **When there is just one trump out higher than yours, it is normally best to leave it out.**

When an opponent has the best trump, it will score sooner or later. To remove it may cost you two trumps and give up the initiative.

WEST	EAST	
♠ A K Q 7 3	♠ 6	West is in 5♣ and ruffs the
♡ 5	♡ J 6 4 2	second heart. The ♣A-♣K
◇ A K	◇ 9 7 5 2	sees North show out on the
♣ A K 6 4 2	♣ 8 7 5 3	second round. What now?

Abandon trumps and start on the spades. Ruffing two spades in dummy ensures 5♣. If you play a third trump to remove their top trump, dummy has only one trump left. You would now fail if either opponent had five or more spades.

WEST	EAST	
♠ A 2	♠ J 6	West is in 6♡ and receives the
♡ 9 7 5 3 2	♡ A K 6 4	♠K lead. West takes the ♠A
◇ A 2	◇ K Q J 7 6 5	and cashes the ♡A-♡K. North
♣ A J 5 4	♣ 8	shows out on the second round
		of trumps. What now?

To play a third trump would allow the opponents to cash a spade. Start on diamonds and hope that South began with at least two diamonds. The spade loser can be discarded on the third diamond.

WEST	EAST	
♠ A K 2	♠ J 6	Although 6◇ is safer, West is
♡ K 9 7 5 3 2	♡ A 6	in 6♡ and receives the ♠5
◇ A 2	◇ K Q J 7 6 5	lead: jack – queen – ace. All
♣ A 6	♣ Q 8 3	follow to the ♡A, ♡K. How
		should West continue?

If dummy has a solid suit and no outside entry, ignore the Rule of 1 and clear the last trump. Play a third heart. Otherwise, they may ruff the second or third diamond and cut you off from all the tricks in dummy.

TIP 2:

The Rule of 2: **When you are missing two non-touching honours, it is normally best to finesse first for their *lower* honour.**

WEST	EAST	
7 6 5	A Q 10	For three tricks or the maximum possible, finesse the ten first, not the queen.

The same applies for seven or eight cards between the two hands. With nine or ten cards, finessing the queen is the better chance. Needing only two tricks from A-Q-10 opposite x-x-x or similar, finesse the queen.

WEST	EAST	
8 7 6 4 2	K J 9 5 3	You lead the two and North plays the ten. Do you finesse the jack or the king?

If South has the A-Q, your play is immaterial. If the ace and queen are split, either finesse is a 50% chance. Play the jack because it gains not only when North has Q-10 but also when North began with A-Q-10.

If the ace and the jack are missing, it is normal to finesse for the jack on the second round (in case the jack falls on the first round).

WEST	EAST	
K 7 6 4	Q 10 5 3	Do not lead low to the 10 first. Play the 3 to the king and finesse the 10 next time.

If only one finesse can be taken, finesse for the jack first:

WEST	EAST	
7	K Q 10 8 5 3	For the best chance to lose only one trick, play the seven to the ten.

Ignore the Rule of 2 if you need to keep a specific opponent off lead:

WEST	EAST	
♠ 8 7 6 4 3 2	♠ K J 10 5	West is in 4♠ on a low club
♡ K 5	♡ 7 6 4	lead to the queen and ace.
◇ 8 4 3	◇ A K Q J 2	How should West continue?
♣ A J	♣ 6	

Lead a trump and play dummy's K if North plays the 9. This holds the losers to one if North began with ♠A-9. Even if North started with ♠A-Q-9, the ♡K-5 is protected and you now run diamonds. If you finesse the J and lose to Q-bare, a heart through the K might beat you.

TIP 3:

The Rule of 3-over-3: **If the bidding has reached the 3-level on a competitive part-score deal, choose to defend unless you know your side has at least a 9-card fit.**

Dealer East : Both vulnerable

WEST	NORTH	EAST	SOUTH
		1♠	2◇
No	No	Dble	No
3♣	No	No	?

What would you do as South now?

SOUTH
♠ K Q 6
♡ J 6 3
◇ A K J 8 6 2
♣ 8

It seems likely that they will make 3♣ but as there is no evidence that your side has nine trumps or more, you should pass and defend. Had West bid 2♡ or 2♠, it would be reasonable to compete to 3◇ rather than sell out at the 2-level. As the bidding is already at the 3-level, defending is the recommended action, with no evidence of a trump fit for your side. If you bid 3◇ over 3♣, you deserve this layout:

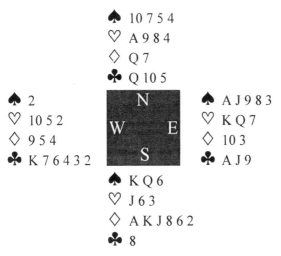

```
              ♠ 10 7 5 4
              ♡ A 9 8 4
              ◇ Q 7
              ♣ Q 10 5
♠ 2                         ♠ A J 9 8 3
♡ 10 5 2          N         ♡ K Q 7
◇ 9 5 4       W       E     ◇ 10 3
♣ K 7 6 4 3 2     S         ♣ A J 9
              ♠ K Q 6
              ♡ J 6 3
              ◇ A K J 8 6 2
              ♣ 8
```

West would lead the ♠2 and the play is likely to go: ♠A; ♠3, ruffed; club to the ace; ♠9, ruffed; heart exit and South will be two down, –200, instead of –110 or –130 defending against 3♣. If stronger, West might double 3◇.

When should you compete above them at the 3-level?

1. When you have a trump fit with nine or more trumps between you.

2. When your side has a clear strength advantage, such as 23 HCP v. 17.

Even then do not compete to the 4-level with only part-score values.

WEST	NORTH	EAST	SOUTH	SOUTH	
No	No	1♦	1♠	♠	A J 8 7 6 4
Dble*	2♠	3♡	?	♡	7
What would you do as South now?				♦	K J 3
*For takeout, promises 4+ hearts				♣	6 4 3

South knows that North-South have at least nine trumps and with a shortage in hearts and well-placed diamonds, South has a clear-cut 3♠ bid despite the meagre point count. Some might even jump to 4♠ as an advance sacrifice but there is nothing to say that East-West intend to bid 4♡.

WEST	NORTH	EAST	SOUTH	SOUTH	
		No	No	♠	K Q 7
1♦	1♠	2♡	2♠	♡	J 10 3
3♡	No	No	?	♦	A 9 5 2
What should South do?				♣	7 6 3

The evidence indicates that North-South do not have nine trumps, as North declined to bid 3♠ despite South's support. South has no shortage and so no ruffing values. South should pass 3♡.

WEST	NORTH	EAST	SOUTH	SOUTH	
	No	1♦	No	♠	8 2
1♠	No	2♠	No	♡	9 7
No	Dble	3♠	?	♦	9 4 3
What should South do now?				♣	K Q J 8 7 6

North's double was purely competitive, aimed at pushing East-West one level higher and giving the defence a better chance for a plus score. North has succeeded in that objective. With a decent hand, North would have bid earlier. South should pass. Do not compete to the 4-level on a part-score deal.

TIP 4:

The Rule of 4-4: **Delay showing support for partner's 5-card suit if a superior 4-4 fit might be available.**

A good 4-4 fit may enable you to make extra tricks by using the 5-3, 5-4 or 6-4 side fit for discards.

WEST	EAST	WEST	EAST
♠ A Q 5 2	♠ K 8 7 4	1♡	1♠
♡ K Q 8 5 2	♡ A J 4 3	3♠	4♠
◇ A 3	◇ J 2	No	
♣ 5 2	♣ Q 7 4		

East's 1♠ rather than a limit 3♡ raise led to 4♠, which can make 11 tricks if spades are 3-2. The normal maximum in hearts is ten tricks. If spades are 4-1, 4♠ may yet make while 4♡ is very likely to fail.

WEST	EAST	WEST	EAST
♠ K J 8 7 4	♠ A Q 2	1♠ *	2♣
♡ A Q 5 2	♡ K J 4 3	2♡	4♡
◇ A 4	◇ 9 6 5	No	
♣ 8 5	♣ A 7 3	*Playing 5-card majors	

By temporizing with 2♣, East found the superior heart contract. With spades as trumps or in no-trumps, the limit is eleven tricks but twelve tricks can be made in hearts if they divide 3-2.

WEST	EAST	WEST	EAST
♠ K Q 5 3	♠ A 8 7 6 4 2	1♣ *	1♠
♡ A 2	♡ 9 4	?	
◇ A J 5	◇ 6	*Playing Precision, where the 1♣	
♣ K 10 4 2	♣ A Q J 5	opening is artificial and strong	

The 1♠ response showed a 5+ suit and 8+ HCP. What should West do next?

If West supports spades, East-West are likely to reach 6♠ (or 6NT). If West marks time, say, with 1NT, the club fit can be discovered and perhaps the excellent grand slam in clubs can be found.

TIP 5:

The Rule of 5-over-5: **When the bidding has reached the 5-level in a competitive auction, it is usually better to defend than to bid on.**

Suppose the bidding has started:

WEST	NORTH	EAST	SOUTH
1♡	1♠	3♡	3♠
4♡	4♠	5♡	No
No	?		

What action should North take?

If you are the weaker side and your sacrificial 4♠ has pushed them to the 5-level, be satisfied with that. Perhaps you can defeat them when they would have succeeded one level lower. That is your profit for having pushed them one higher. Bid 5♠ and your good work might be completely undone.

If you are the stronger side, it is normally better to accept the penalty than to bid higher and risk defeat. Of course, if you are the stronger side, you will double their sacrifice. To bid 5-over-5 you need to be almost certain that your contract will succeed, in other words, that your side is close to making a slam.

The more balanced your hand, the less attractive it is to push higher. High cards in their suit strongly suggest defending. A void in their suit, or even a singleton, is one factor in favour of bidding on. Likewise a holding of four cards in their suit would strongly suggest that partner has a singleton or void there. The worst holding with which to bid more is a useless doubleton in their suit.

If unable to tell which side has the greater strength, definitely defend but you do not need to double. On many occasions neither side can succeed at the 5-level. You might well have been beaten at the 4-level.

Tip 3 (defend at the 3-level) and Tip 5 (defend at the 5-level) are summed up by this memory guide:

Defend on odd occasions.

TIP 6:

The Rule of 6, Part 1: **A 6-card suit is shown when responder bids 1NT and later follows with a change of suit.**

WEST	EAST	
1♠	1NT	In these auctions East is denying any support or
2♡	3♣	tolerance for opener's suits. East is likely to have
		5-8 HCP and normally a 6-card suit or longer.

WEST	EAST	
1♠	1NT	This would be certain if responder's rebid is at
2♢	2♡	the 3-level and it is a sensible approach when
		responder rebids at the 2-level.

Responder would pass the second suit with three cards there and give preference to the first suit, known to be a 5+ suit, with doubleton support. With at most three cards in opener's suits responder is highly likely to have a 6+ suit (although a 5-5-2-1 pattern is possible).

Opener should usually pass this new suit rebid. To bid again opener needs a 6-5 pattern or support for responder's suit. Neither 2NT nor 3NT is a rescue haven. Do not expect responder to have 9+ HCP. With that, responder has enough to bid and rebid the 6-card suit.

If opener rebids the suit opened (e.g., 1♠ : 1NT, 2♠), opener should have a 6+ suit and responder will normally pass. When should responder remove this to a long suit at the 3-level? Use this guide:

The Rule of 6, Part 2: **After a 1NT response, if opener rebids at the two-level in the suit opened, responder subtracts the number of cards held in opener's suit from the number of cards in responder's long suit. If the answer is *below 6*, pass. If the answer is *6 or more*, bid three of your long suit.**

Suppose the bidding starts 1♡ : 1NT, 2♡ and responder holds:

(1) ♠ K 6	(2) ♠ K 6 5	(3) ♠ 8 7
♡ 7	♡ - - -	♡ 7
♢ A 8 7 4 3 2	♢ A 8 7 4 3 2	♢ K Q 9 7 6 3 2
♣ 7 6 5 2	♣ 7 6 5 2	♣ J 10 2

(1) Pass. Difference is 5 (6 diamonds minus 1 heart).
(2) Bid 3♢. Difference is 6 (6 diamonds minus 0 hearts).
(3) Bid 3♢. Difference is 6 (7 diamonds minus 1 heart).

TIP 7:

The Rule of 7: **In no-trumps, when you intend to hold up with only one stopper in the enemy suit, add the number of cards held by you and dummy in that suit and deduct the total from 7. The answer is the number of times you should duck.**

With five cards in the enemy suit, duck twice. (7 − 5 = 2). With six cards, duck once and with seven, do not duck at all. This clever rule appeared in *Step by Step Card Play in No-trumps* by Robert Berthe and Norbert Lebely. It is very useful if you intend to hold up anyway.

(1) NORTH	(2) NORTH	(3) NORTH
♠ A Q J 10	♠ A Q J 10	♠ A Q J 2
♡ A 8 4 2	♡ A 4 2	♡ 9 8
◇ 10 6	◇ 10 2	◇ 10 6 2
♣ 7 4 3	♣ 7 6 4 3	♣ K J 4 2
SOUTH	SOUTH	SOUTH
♠ K 5 4	♠ K 5 4	♠ 7 5 4
♡ K 9 6	♡ 9 6 3	♡ K 5
◇ A 8 3	◇ A 4 3	◇ A 8 3
♣ K Q J 2	♣ A Q J 2	♣ A Q 8 7 3

In each case the ◇5 is led and East plays the ◇K. Plan your play.

(1) The Rule of 7 says to duck twice. There is no reason to do otherwise. Take the ◇A on the third round and play to set up club winners. If West began with 5+ diamonds and East has the ♣A, all will be well.

(2) The Rule of 7 says to duck twice but that is unwise here. If you let East hold the trick, a heart switch might see you undone if you have to lose a trick in clubs to bring your trick tally to nine. If the ◇5 lead is fourth-highest, West has four diamonds only. The lower diamonds are all visible. Take the ◇A and play to set up two club tricks. At pairs, take the club finesse. At teams, cash the ♣A, cross to dummy with a spade and lead a club. This caters for ♣K singleton with West.

(3) The Rule of 7 says to duck twice, but you must not duck at all. The risk of a heart switch is too great. The best chance is to take the ◇A and take the spade finesse, repeating it if successful.

16

TIP 8:

The Rule of 8, Part 1: **With eight cards including A, K and J, it is usually best to finesse for the Q on the second round of the suit.**

(1) WEST	EAST		(2) WEST	EAST
A K J 7	6 5 3 2		A K J 7 4	5 3 2

(3) WEST	EAST		(4) WEST	EAST
A K J 7 5 4	3 2		A K J 10 7 4	3 2

In (1), (2) and (3), cash the ace (in case the queen is singleton), cross to East and lead low to the jack on the second round.

In (4) it is better to cross to East, finesse the jack, return to East and finesse the ten. If the suit breaks 3-2 or South has a singleton, cashing the ace first makes no difference. If North has a singleton, then cashing the ace first gains when the singleton is the queen. Taking two finesses gains when North has a singleton 9, 8, 6 or 5. That makes taking two finesses four times more likely to succeed than ace first.

The Rule of 8, Part 2: **With eight cards including K, Q and 10, it is usually best to finesse for the J on the second round of the suit.**

(5) WEST	EAST		(6) WEST	EAST
K Q 10 4	6 5 3 2		K 7 4	Q 10 5 3 2

(7) WEST	EAST		(8) WEST	EAST
K Q 5 4	10 7 3 2		K Q 10 9 6 4	3 2

In (5), (6) and (7), start by leading low from East to West's king. For (5) and (6), whether the king wins or loses, continue by leading low to the ten on the next round. In (7), the ten is not part of a tenace and so there is no finesse of the 10. If the king wins, return to East and lead towards the queen. If the king loses, cash the queen next.

For (8), cross to East, then finesse the 10, return to East and finesse the 9. This gains against J-x-x-x or A-J-x-x with South.

The above rules refer only to the correct handling of one suit. There may be other considerations for the management of the whole hand.

TIP 9:

The Rule of 9, Part 1: **With nine cards including A, K and J, it is slightly better to play the A and K and hope that the queen falls than to finesse the J on the second round.**

(1) WEST	EAST	(2) WEST	EAST
A K J 7 4	6 5 3 2	A K 5 4 2	J 10 6 3

(3) WEST	EAST	(4) WEST	EAST
A 7 5 4 2	K J 9 3	A 10 8 4 3	K J 5 2

In (1) and (2), play the ace and continue with the king.

(3) Play the ace first. If all follow, play to the king next. Do not start with the king. Cashing the ace allows you to avoid any loser if North began with Q-10-8-6 by virtue of East's jack and nine. If South has Q-10-8-6, two tricks will lost however you play.

(4) Play low to the king first. This gains if South began with Q-9-7-6. You can then avoid a loser, thanks to West's ten and eight. If North began with Q-9-7-6, one trick has to be lost.

By all means dispense with the Rule of 9 when there are more important considerations:

WEST	EAST	
♠ K J 10 4 2	♠ A 7 6 3	West is in 6♠ with no opposition
♡ Q 10	♡ A K	bidding. The lead is the ♡6. How
◇ A J 6	◇ K 5 2	would you plan the play as West?
♣ A K 10	♣ Q 7 5 3	

You would be unlucky to fail if you play the ♠A and ♠K at tricks 2 and 3, but if the ♠Q does not drop, you will need four tricks from the clubs or, failing that, the diamond finesse. You can improve greatly on this line, making the slam close to a certainty. Take the ♡A and cash the ♠A. If both follow low, cash the ♡K and then play a low spade. If South shows out, rise with the ♠K and exit with a spade. North wins but no matter which suit is played, your potential loser in diamonds will vanish.

If South follows to the second spade, finesse the ♠J. If it wins, you are home and if it loses to ♠Q doubleton, North is again end-played.

If North shows out on the first spade, finesse the ♠J, return to dummy with a heart and repeat the spade finesse. Draw the last trump and try for an overtrick. It is only when South shows out on the first spade that you will need to develop an extra trick in the minors.

The Rule of 9, Part 2: **With nine cards including K, Q and 10, it is slightly better to play for the J to drop than to finesse the 10 on the second round.**

WEST	EAST	
Q 10 7 4 2	K 6 5 3	Lead low to the K. If that loses to the A, play the Q later and hope that the J drops.

The Rule of 9, Part 3: **With nine cards including A, K and 10, cash the ace or king first, retaining the A-10 or K-10 as a tenace. If the queen or jack falls from the hand sitting over the tenace, play for the honour card to be singleton, not from Q-J doubleton.**

WEST	EAST	
K 7 5 4 2	A 10 6 3	Cash the king first, the winner opposite the tenace, not the ace first.

If both follow low or North produces an honour, continue with a low card to the ace. If South played the jack or queen under your king, play low to dummy's ten next. This is your best chance to avoid a loser. You are hoping North began with Q-9-8 or J-9-8. You need strong reasons to play contrary to Part 3.

The question whether it is better in general to play for the drop or to finesse for any missing honour card can be determined by the Even Suit Break (see Tip 56). It is most important to appreciate that the best play of a complete hand may require an approach different from the usual technique in handling a single suit.

TIP 10:

The Rule of 10-10: **When you have a 10-card trump fit and one of the partnership hands has ten cards in two suits, the playing strength is far greater than the high card values suggest.**

Teams : South dealer : North-South vulerable

WEST	NORTH	EAST	SOUTH
			No
1 ◇	1 ♠	Dble*	2 ♣
No	?	*6+ points, 4+ hearts	

NORTH
♠ A K 5 4 3
♡ 4
◇ A Q 4
♣ Q 8 3 2

What should North do with these cards:

In a tournament to select a national team most raised only to 3♣, a feeble effort indeed. North has 15 HCP, four-card support (the raise to 3♣ might be with just three trumps), a useful singleton, the ◇ A-Q over the opening bidder's suit and only five losers. A minimum overcall usually has eight losers and a maximum has six. That means North has a super-maximum overcall once the club fit comes to light.

North is worth a 3♡ splinter bid, which would show the shortage, confirm the extra trump length and show a stronger hand than 3♣. If the splinter raise is not available, 4♣ would be reasonable.

Only one North-South pair of six reached game, but 6♣ was on:

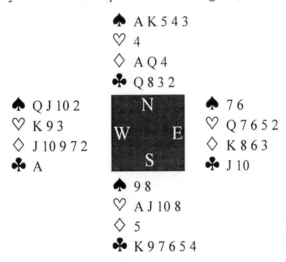

```
                 ♠ A K 5 4 3
                 ♡ 4
                 ◇ A Q 4
                 ♣ Q 8 3 2
  ♠ Q J 10 2          N          ♠ 7 6
  ♡ K 9 3                        ♡ Q 7 6 5 2
  ◇ J 10 9 7 2    W       E      ◇ K 8 6 3
  ♣ A                 S          ♣ J 10
                 ♠ 9 8
                 ♡ A J 10 8
                 ◇ 5
                 ♣ K 9 7 6 5 4
```

TIPS 11-20: Constructive bidding

TIP 11:

You know it, you go it

As soon as you are aware of the correct contract, bid it forthwith. Do not take partner – and the opponents – on a scenic tour to see all the wonders of your hand if the final destination is known. It is necessary to give partner information when you are not yet certain of the best spot, but once you do know, it is best to go straight to it.

Suppose partner opened 1♢, you respond 1♡ and partner rebids 2♢. What action would you take next with:

♠ A Q 9 2   ♡ K Q 6 4   ♢ 7   ♣ A 6 5 4

Failing to heed the above advice cost on this deal:

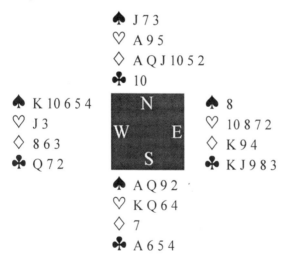

```
              ♠ J 7 3
              ♡ A 9 5
              ♢ A Q J 10 5 2
              ♣ 10
♠ K 10 6 5 4      N        ♠ 8
♡ J 3                      ♡ 10 8 7 2
♢ 8 6 3       W       E    ♢ K 9 4
♣ Q 7 2           S        ♣ K J 9 8 3
              ♠ A Q 9 2
              ♡ K Q 6 4
              ♢ 7
              ♣ A 6 5 4
```

In a teams match one South bid 3NT over 2♢, which had denied four spades. West led a spade, won by South who took the losing diamond finesse. The switch to clubs came but South had eleven tricks.

At the other table South bid a futile 2♠ over 2♢ and rebid 3NT over North's 3♡. Here West led a club and declarer was one down.

TIP 12:

Do not be afraid to bid a weak 4-card suit at the one-level, whether you are the opener or the responder.

(a) The correct contract may be in your suit:

WEST	EAST	WEST	EAST
♠ A 8 7 6	♠ 9 5 4 2	1♦	1♠
♡ Q 3	♡ K 8 6	2♠	No
♢ A K 7 6 4	♢ 5 2		
♣ 8 2	♣ A 7 6 4		

The best contract for East-West is likely to be in spades, reached easily if East responds 1♠. If East in trepidation replies 1NT, West might pass or rebid 2♢, both significantly inferior to 2♠, where eight or nine tricks are likely. West is too weak to reverse into 2♠ and so if the partnership is to find the spade fit, it is up to East to bid them first. A good guide for responder is to *reply 1NT only as a last resort.*

(b) Bidding a weak 4-card suit may keep the opponents out of their best contract. It may also ward off a lead in that suit if the final contract is in some other denomination.

(c) If no-trumps is the correct spot, it is often better for the strong opener to be declarer rather than the weak responder.

WEST	EAST	WEST	EAST
♠ A 3	♠ 7 5 4 2	1♦	1♠
♡ A Q 3	♡ 8 5 4	2NT	3NT
♢ K Q J 8	♢ 10 7 3	No	
♣ Q J 5 2	♣ A K 4		

The best contract is 3NT by West, but if East responds 1NT, West will raise to 3NT. Now a heart lead goes through the tenace and 3NT may fail, while 3NT is secure on a heart lead if West is declarer. The spade response allows West to bid the no-trumps first.

If East responds 1NT, South might lead a spade, which could also be fatal, while the 1♠ response may inhibit the spade lead. If possible, the weaker hand should not snatch a possible no-trump contract from the stronger hand.

TIP 13:

Repeat a 5-card suit only as a last resort, whether you are the opener or the responder.

One of the worst concepts inflicted on bridgekind was the 'rebiddable suit'. While the idea has merit in indicating when one might rebid a suit, it has been widely misinterpreted so that rebidding a 5-card suit became an obligation. 'Rebiddable' means 'able to be rebid', not 'forced to rebid'. More bidding sins are committed under the excuse, 'I has to show you I had five, partner' than in any other single area.

Problems for opener:

If you have opened with a suit at the one-level and partner responds with the cheapest bid, repeating your suit will normally promise a 6-card suit. In auctions like 1 ♢ : 1 ♡, 2 ♢ or 1 ♡ : 1 ♠, 2 ♡ opener is expected to have at least a 6-card suit. If you do not have a 6-card suit you can bid a second suit or rebid 1NT as long as that does not show more points than you have. In desperation you may rebid a very strong 5-card suit (should contain at least three honours) or rebid in a lower-ranking 3-card suit.

Suppose the bidding has started 1 ♡ : 1 ♠. What would you rebid with each of these hands:

(1) ♠	A 9 5	(2) ♠	A 2	(3) ♠	9 3
♡	K 8 7 4 2	♡	K Q J 10 2	♡	A 8 6 4 3
♢	7 3	♢	7 3 2	♢	K 5 2
♣	K Q 3	♣	K 9 4	♣	A Q 2

(1) You could rebid 1NT as long as that does not show 15+ points. If 1NT is not available, bid 2 ♠ and even if 1NT is an option, 2 ♠ is a sensible move, since you have a ruffing value outside.

(2) If 1NT is not available, rebid 2 ♡. You have only five hearts but a 5-card suit with four honours is as good as a 6-card suit.

(3) The hearts are much too weak to rebid and if 1NT is not possible, your best shot is a 2 ♣ rebid. This is not ideal but it is the best choice. Because of problems such as these, many players would open these hands with a weak 1NT.

Where the response is beyond the cheapest bid, opener may be forced to rebid a 5-card suit. A new suit rebid by opener beyond 2-of-the-suit-opened is a strong rebid, a 'reverse', normally 16+ points. If weaker than that, opener may have to repeat a 5-card suit.

OPENER	After 1♣ : 1◇, opener will rebid 1♡ but after
♠ 3	1♣ : 1♠, opener is too weak to rebid 2♡ and
♡ K J 5 2	so is forced into a 2♣ rebid. If a 1NT rebid does
◇ K 3 2	not promise 15+ points, many would choose that
♣ A J 7 5 2	rather than rebid the clubs.

There are two distinct situations for responder:

1. If your rebid would not be forcing, be extremely reluctant to rebid a 5-card suit. Do it only as a last resort and check that you have not overlooked any other reasonable option. Suppose you hold:

♠ 7 6   ♡ A 8 7 6 3   ◇ K 8 4   ♣ 9 7 3

Partner has opened 1♣ and you responded 1♡. What is your rebid if partner rebids (a) 1♠?   (b) 2◇?

What if partner opened 1◇ and you responded 1♡? What is your rebid if partner rebids (c) 2♣?   (d) 1♠?

(a) After 1♣ : 1♡, 1♠, rebid 1NT. The 5-3-3-2 is a balanced pattern and there is no reason to expect hearts to be a better spot.

(b) Rebid 3♣, giving preference to partner's first suit. As opener has reversed, opener's first suit should be longer than the second. Clubs is a known trump fit, hearts an unknown quantity.

(c) Rebid 2◇, the known fit, giving preference to opener's first suit.

(d) Rebid 1NT or give preference to 2◇ rather than rebid the hearts.

2. If you are in a game-forcing auction, you may rebid your 5-card suit freely below game to explore the best spot. If the bidding has started 1◇ : 1♠, 2NT (forcing) by all means rebid 3♠ on a 5-card suit. In the same auction, if you have five spades and four hearts, rebid 3♡, not 3♠, so that the game in the right strain can be reached.

TIP 14:

Be prepared to rescue partner once but not twice.

When searching for a decent part-score, you often have little space in which to manoeuvre because the partnership strength may be quite limited and you want to bail out as early as possible. Suppose you hold:

♠ 6 4   ♡ 5   ◇ A Q 8 7 4   ♣ A K 7 5 2

The bidding has started 1◇ : 1♠, 2♣ : 2♠. What would you do now?

Partner's 2♠ rebid will normally be based on a 6-card suit (although a very strong 5-card suit is feasible) and you should pass.

What if partner's bid and rebid suit had been hearts? Would you also pass 2♡? With the hand given, you should certainly pass 2♡ because your values in the minor suits will take tricks also in a heart contract. Your cards figure to be more useful to partner in hearts than partner's values will be to you in a minor suit contract. In addition, there is the benefit of staying at the 2-level. When the decision is close, prefer not to push on to three.

However, suppose your hand looked like this:

♠ ---   ♡ 5 3 2   ◇ A Q 8 7 4   ♣ A K 7 5 2

and the bidding has started 1◇ : 1♠, 2♣ : 2♠. What now over 2♠?

While you are entitled to pass, it is not appealing with a void. A rebid of 3♣ is indicated. Partner is expected to pass 3♣ or correct to 3◇ but if partner persists with 3♠, you must pass. Do not consider 3NT as an option with a weak hand after this sequence, even if you had a stopper in hearts. Firstly, you have warned partner by your retreat to 3♣ that you have no tolerance for spades (you would definitely have passed 2♠ with doubleton support and should usually do so also with a singleton). Secondly, if 3♠ is a disaster, you hope it will be a salutary lesson and partner will be wiser for the future.

Other sequences where you should not rescue partner again:
(1) 1♠ : 2♣, 2♠ : 2NT, 3♠ : 3NT . . . Leave partner in 3NT.
(2) 1NT : 2♡ (weakness takeout), 2NT . . . Leave partner in 2NT.
(3) 1♡ : 1NT, 2♡ : 3♣, 3♡ . . . Leave partner in 3♡.

TIP 15:

Choice of contract Part 1: **When you have a choice of two trump suits, prefer to play in the trump suit of the weaker hand and have the stronger hand as dummy.**

It can be more attractive to have the stronger hand as declarer and the weaker hand as dummy but the over-riding consideration is to be in the right contract. Being in the best spot comes first. Having the strong hand as declarer is not nearly as important. Of course, if your methods allow you to be in the right spot and have the opening lead come up to the strong hand, so much the better.

In auctions where the partners seem to be 'fighting' about the trump suit, the stronger hand should usually give way. The strong hand will almost always be more useful with side tricks to the weak hand than vice versa. The strong hand produces the high card tricks, the weak hand has trump winners. Often you will find that the weak hand produces no tricks if the hand is played in the trump suit of the strong hand. Take these hands for example:

WEST	EAST	WEST	EAST
♠ A Q 7 6 5 4	♠ - - -	1♠	1NT
♡ 3	♡ Q J 10 9 6 5	2♣	2♡
◇ Q 10	◇ 9 8 6 4 2	?	
♣ K Q 9 2	♣ A 5		

What action should West take?

Seeing both hands it is not too tough to pass. At the table, it is not as easy to 'see' and it is tempting to rebid 2♠.

West should pass. Firstly, West should figure that as East has at least six hearts (see Tip #6), spades may be a worse trump suit than hearts or, at the best, about equal. Secondly, if the decision is at all close, the tip is to play in the trump suit of the weaker hand.

If spades are trumps, the East hand is worth one trick. If hearts are trumps, the East hand is worth at least five tricks (four hearts and the ♣A). East should make 2♡ easily with one spade, three clubs and four hearts while 2♠ would be in severe jeopardy.

26

Choice of contract Part 2: **When the bulk of your high card strength is in your short suits, or is opposite partner's known short suit, prefer to play in no-trumps.**

Suppose the bidding has started 1♣ by you, 1♠ from partner. What would you rebid with each of these hands?

(1) ♠ A Q	(2) ♠ 7 2	(3) ♠ 8
♡ J 8 7 2	♡ A J 8 2	♡ A Q J
◇ K J	◇ 7 3	◇ K Q J 8
♣ Q 9 7 4 3	♣ A K 9 6 4	♣ 8 7 5 4 3

(1) With 10 of your 13 HCP in your short suits, rebid 1NT rather than 2♣ on such a rotten suit. If playing a weak 1NT, you need to foresee the problem and open 1NT rather than 1♣.

(2) Rebid 2♣. Your long suit is strong, the short suits are pathetic. This indicates you should choose a suit contract.

(3) Rebid 1NT, despite the singleton, rather than 2♣ on such a feeble suit. If playing a 1NT opening as weak, where a 1NT rebid would indicate 15+ points, you must foresee the problem and open 1◇, intending to rebid 2♣ over 1♠.

WEST	EAST	WEST	EAST
♠ Q 5 3	♠ J 8 7 6 4	1◇	1♠
♡ 6	♡ A K J	2♣	2NT
◇ A K J 10 5	◇ 7 3	3♠	3NT
♣ K Q 9 6	♣ J 4 2	No	

With so much strength opposite partner's singleton or void, East judges that 3NT is likely to be easier than 4♠ despite the 5-3 fit. You would be lucky to make 4♠ while 3NT should be easy.

WEST	EAST	WEST	EAST
♠ A Q J	♠ 4	1◇	3♠*
♡ 7 5 3 2	♡ Q J 4	3NT	No
◇ A 9 8 4 3	◇ K Q 7 6 2	*Splinter, 4+ diamonds and	
♣ J	♣ K Q 7 5	short in spades	

With excess strength facing the short suit, West chooses 3NT, which should be routine, while 5◇ might fail even if East had the ♣A.

TIP 16:

With a strong trump fit (or a self-sufficient trump suit), a grand slam is likely if you have no losers in the first three rounds of any suit. If either partner holds a void, a grand slam is feasible with about 27 HCP in the other three suits.

WEST	
♠ A Q 10 7 6	Partner opens 1♣ and raises 1♠ to 2♠. How should you proceed?
♡ A Q 10	
◇ K Q 5	Simply check on aces and kings. If partner has two aces and two kings, bid 7NT. If any of those four cards are missing, stop in 6♠.
♣ K 3	

Corollary to Tip 16: If you are unable to account for the first three rounds of every suit, be content to play for a sound small slam.

WEST	
♠ A K 8 3	Partner opens 1♠. How should you proceed?
♡ A K 7 5	Suppose you find partner has the two missing aces. What next?
◇ K 7	
♣ K J 2	

Unless your methods are able to establish considerably more than that, you should be content with 6♠ or 6NT. Four aces and four kings are only eight tricks. It would be foolish to bid a grand slam and find partner has ♠ Q J 7 6 4 ♡ 9 8 3 ◇ A Q ♣ A Q 7. A grand slam is also poor odds opposite ♠ 9 7 6 5 2   ♡ Q J 2 ◇ A Q 4 ♣ A Q.

To bring greater accuracy to the slam department, many partnerships have adopted Roman Key Card Blackwood (RKCB), which locates not only aces and kings but also the trump honours. In reply to 4NT:

5♣ = 0 or 3 key cards
5◇ = 1 or 4 key cards
5♡ = 2 key cards but not the trump queen
5♠ = 2 key cards plus the trump queen
5NT = 5 key cards, no trump queen
6♣ = 5 key cards plus the trump queen

The key cards are the four aces and the king of the agreed trump suit.

If no trump suit has been specifically agreed, take the last bid suit as the trump suit set. After the 5♣ and 5♢ replies, the cheapest suit excluding trumps asks, 'Do you have the trump queen?' In reply, the cheapest bid = 'No', cheapest plus one = 'Yes'. After the reply to 4NT or the reply to the trump queen ask, 5NT asks for kings outside trumps. In reply, 6♣ = 0, 6♢ = 1, 6♡ = 2 and 6♠ = 3.

WEST	EAST	WEST	EAST
♠ A K Q J 10 7 6	♠ 4		1♢
♡ A 8	♡ Q 6 2	2♠	3♢
♢ A 4 3	♢ K Q J 6 5 2	4NT	5♠
♣ 6	♣ A 7 2	7NT	No

4NT = RKCB, setting diamonds, the last bid suit, as trumps.
5♠ showed two key cards (♣A and ♢K) plus the ♢Q.

If partner is known to hold a void, the high cards opposite the void are often wasted. On the other hand, if you have no high cards opposite the void, slam can be made with modest high card values.

WEST	EAST	WEST	EAST
♠ A 8 6 4	♠ K Q 9 7 2	1♣	1♠
♡ K 4 3 2	♡ A Q 6	3♢	3♡ --- cue-bid
♢ - - -	♢ 8 7 5	4♢	4NT --- RKCB
♣ K Q 8 6 3	♣ A 7	5♢	5NT --- Kings?
		6♡	7♠

3♢ was a splinter raise of spades (4+ spades, shortage in diamonds, enough for at least 3♠). After the 3♡ cue, 4♢ = diamond void. After finding one ace and two kings, East knew enough to bid 7♠.

With lots of strength facing the void, beware of heading for slam unless you know you have at least 25 HCP *outside the void*.

WEST	EAST	WEST	EAST
♠ A 8 6 4	♠ K Q 9 7 2	1♣	1♠
♡ - - -	♡ A Q 6	3♡	4♣ --- cue-bid
♢ K 4 3 2	♢ 8 7 5	4♡	4♠
♣ K Q 8 6 3	♣ A 7	No	

When 4♡ showed the void, East's values plummeted. With extra values, West could continue over 4♠ as 4♣ showed slam interest.

TIP 17:

When the opponents clearly have enough for game or a slam, be prepared to make a psychic bid if your side has an excellent trump fit or if the vulnerability is favourable.

Suppose partner opens 2♠ (weak two, 6-card suit, 6-10 HCP) and next player passes. What action would you take with:

♠ K 8 7 5 2   ♡ 8 7   ◇ 4   ♣ Q 9 5 4 2

The opponents have at least 25 HCP and probably more. As partner should not have four cards in the other major, the opponents hold at least eight hearts. Similarly, as partner would not have five diamonds, the opponents also have at least eight diamonds. The opponents can make a game and quite probably a slam. You have no reasonable prospects for a defensive trick. Partner may or may not have a trick.

With this knowledge you must take some action before the opponents locate their fit and strength. At the very least bid 4♠. This will fail but will be a cheap sacrifice. Against naive opponents 4NT Blackwood may silence them, even though you subside in 5♠ after discovering that partner lacks the aces for a slam! Except at unfavourable vulnerability, 5♠ doubled should be cheaper than their game or slam.

Against sophisticated opponents a more subtle approach might work. How about a 2NT response, which is used to initiate a game or slam try and invariably implies a strong hand? The drawback to 2NT is that it allows fourth player cheap action at the 3-level.

If you are prepared to be downright brazen, try a bid of 3♡, played as natural, strong and forcing after a weak two. If fourth player doubles this, is it for takeout or for penalties? Many partnerships will not have defined the meaning of double in this auction. What would 3♠ or 4♡ by them mean? If right-hand opponent passes the double, you can retreat, first to 3NT and ultimately to 4♠.

Another neat move is 4♡, normally played as a natural sign-off. If everybody passes, you can afford ten off undoubled at favourable vulnerability and still show a profit. If doubled, you hightail it back to 4♠. They may still find their game but miss their slam.

Dealer West : North-South vulnerable

West	North	East	South
No	No	?	

What action would you take with:

♠ 5 3   ♡ 9 8 7 4   ◇ J 10 5 2   ♣ 9 6 5

No one could criticise a pass. After all, you have only one jack but passing indicates victim mentality. With partner a passed hand, the opponents have enough for game and quite possibly a slam. At this favourable vulnerability a psyche is unlikely to cost.

Once you decide to bid, what is best? Bid where you have some values (1◇ here) and prefer a minor, as that is less likely to enthuse partner than a major suit. The deal arose in a national selection event:

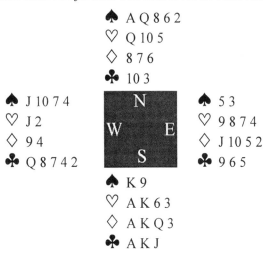

```
              ♠ A Q 8 6 2
              ♡ Q 10 5
              ◇ 8 7 6
              ♣ 10 3
♠ J 10 7 4         N           ♠ 5 3
♡ J 2                          ♡ 9 8 7 4
◇ 9 4       W           E      ◇ J 10 5 2
♣ Q 8 7 4 2       S            ♣ 9 6 5
              ♠ K 9
              ♡ A K 6 3
              ◇ A K Q 3
              ♣ A K J
```

Twelve pairs made a small slam and four bid 7NT, one failing. Two pairs stopped in 3NT. This was the auction at one of those tables:

West	North	East	South	
No	No	2◇*	Dble	
No	2♠	No	3NT	End

*Weak two in diamonds

Both North and South might have done more, but the actual outcome was a victory for East's enterprise.

TIP 18:

The concept of a 'reverse bid' ceases to apply if opener is obliged to bid and the bidding has progressed beyond two of opener's suit before opener has had a chance to rebid.

Opener's reverse is a new suit rebid at the 2-level with the second suit higher-ranking than the suit opened, such as 1♣ : 1♠, 2♥. The reverse promises a strong opening (16+ HCP or 5 losers or fewer) and two suits of unequal length, the first bid suit being the longer.

For each of these hands, the bidding has begun 1♣ by you and 1♠ from partner. What is your rebid?

(1)	♠	3 2	(2)	♠	3	(3)	♠	3 2
	♥	A J 5 4		♥	A J 5 4		♥	A J 5 4
	♦	3 2		♦	A 3 2		♦	A Q 3
	♣	A K J 4 2		♣	A K J 4 2		♣	A K J 4

(1) Rebid 2♣. The shape is right for 2♥ but the hand is too weak.
(2) Rebid 2♥. Shape and strength are right for the reverse.
(3) Jump in no-trumps. Do not reverse with a balanced hand.

If the bidding has progressed beyond two of opener's suit, a new suit rebid at the 2-level does not promise extra strength or suits of unequal length if opener is forced to bid.

WEST	WEST	EAST	
♠ A J 7 3	1♣	2♦	West should rebid 2♥. This does not count as a reverse. The bidding
♥ K Q 4 2	?		is taken as though it had started
♦ 6			1♣ : 1♦ and 2♥ over 2♦ is the
♣ K 8 4 3			same as 1♥ over 1♦.

WEST	WEST	NORTH	EAST	SOUTH
♠ 7 3	1♣	1♠	2♦	No
♥ A Q 8 6	?			
♦ A 3	West should rebid 2♥. The bidding has bypassed			
♣ K 7 5 4 2	2♣ and West is forced to bid.			

After 1♣ West, No Bid North, 1♠ East and 2♦ by South, a 2♥ rebid by West is a reverse. Not forced to bid, West should pass 2♦ if weak.

TIP 19:

You may bid a fake suit if (1) partner is known not to hold 4-card support, *or* (2) you have a safe haven if partner does happen to raise the fake suit.

1. *Partner cannot hold support*

WEST	WEST	EAST	EAST A	EAST B
♠ A K 7		1◇	♠ 6 5	♠ Q J 3
♡ K 8 4 3	1♡	3◇	♡ A 2	♡ A 2
◇ J 6 5	?		◇ A Q 10 8 7 3	◇ A K Q 8 7 3
♣ 8 4 3			♣ A Q 2	♣ J 2

West should rebid 3♠. East's 3◇ rebid denies four spades and so East cannot raise to 4♠ (or if East does, West reverts to 5◇). The 3♠ rebid shows values in spades and focusses on the club suit.

With clubs stopped, East can rebid 3NT (East A). If partner has no values in clubs (East B), you will avoid a risky 3NT. East B will rebid 4◇ over 3♠ and West can raise to 5◇.

A similar thread runs through these sequences:

(a)	W	E	(b)	W	E	(c)	W	E	(d)	W	E
	1♣	1◇		1◇	1♡		1◇	1♡		1♣	1♡
	2♣	2♠		2◇	2♠		2♣	2♠		2◇	2♠

In each of these auctions it is safe for East to bid 2♠ without a 4-card suit, as West's 2♣ or 2◇ rebid has denied holding four spades. The 2♠ bid is forcing but the message is not the same in each case.

Where only two suits have been bid, such as (a) and (b), a new suit bid, if fake, shows strength in the suit bid and seeks a stopper in the unbid suit.

Where three suits have been bid, such as (c) and (d), bidding the fourth suit denies values in that suit, for the time being anyway, and asks partner for more information, including whether a stopper is held in that suit for no-trumps. If three suits have been bid, you could bid no-trumps yourself if you had the fourth suit covered.

2. *Partner might hold support*

WEST	EAST
1♦	1♠
2♦	?

EAST
♠ K J 9 8 2
♡ A K
♦ Q 9 3 2
♣ J 2

What should East do with these cards:

When partner cannot hold support, bidding a fake suit is almost risk-free. If partner could hold support, it is risky to bid a suit in which you do not have length. If you do, you must be prepared to deal with the contingency that partner raises the fake suit. As long as you can cope with that problem, or are prepared to risk the consequences, by all means go ahead and bid your fake suit if that seems the best move.

On the problem above, East has no ideal, natural bid. The hand is too strong for 3♦. Take a king away and 3♦ is the value bid. You are worth 4♦ or 5♦, but that may bypass the best spot of 3NT. In addition, partner might have 3-card spade support and the right contract could be 4♠. The clubs are too weak for a 3NT rebid and a jump-rebid of 3♠ would show a 6+ suit.

A sensible move by East is to rebid 2♡. That will imply five spades (as well as four or more hearts). The good news is that partner might have three spades and rebid 2♠ or 3♠. Without spade support, partner might be able to bid 2NT with the clubs stopped and you will raise to 3NT. A hand like this would be suitable for 2NT over 2♡:

♠ Q   ♡ 8 3 2   ♦ A K 10 7 6 4   ♣ K Q 3

The bad news is that West might raise hearts. West could hold 5+ diamonds and 4 hearts but lack the strength to reverse, such as:

♠ 5   ♡ J 8 6 2   ♦ A K 10 7 6 4   ♣ K Q

If West raises only to 3♡, you might try 3♠, hoping partner gets the message that the problem is the club position for no-trumps. If partner perseveres with 4♡, you can revert to 5♦ and pray partner passes.

If West raises to 4♡, you revert to 5♦ and again hope for the best.

34

TIP 20:

With a 6-5 pattern in touching suits, with five cards in the higher-ranking suit, bid the higher-ranking suit first if the suits are weak and you are minimum in high card values. This applies whether you are opener or responder.

With a 6-5 pattern, the normal rule is to open in the longer suit, then bid and rebid the shorter suit. Bid the six, the five, then the five again. When your suits are poor and the hand is a minimum, bid the higher-ranking suit first, even if it is the 5-card suit, when the suits are touching.

A poor suit has two or three losers and includes only one of the top three honours. A strong suit has at least two of the top three honours and preferably at least one other honour.

Examples for opener

     ♠ A Q 7 6 4   ♡ J 8 6 4 3 2   ◇ - - -   ♣ K Q

Weak, long suit, minimum high-card content. Open 1♠ rather than 1♡. If partner fails to support spades, bid and rebid the hearts.

     ♠ A Q J 7 6   ♡ K Q 10 8 4 3   ◇ - - -   ♣ 7 2

Minimum high-card content but excellent suits. Open 1♡, and if hearts are not supported, bid and rebid the spades. After 1♡ : 2♣ / 2◇, you can rebid 2♠ as a reverse despite holding only 12 HCP, because the hand has only four losers and thus excellent playing strength.

Examples for responder

     ♠ Q 2   ♡ Q J 7 4 2   ◇ Q 8 7 6 3 2   ♣ - - -

After a 1♣ opening, respond 1♡, not 1◇. Your suits are poor and the point count is minimum. If partner rebids 2♣, you could pass but you might risk a 2◇ rebid (forcing) and rebid 3◇ if partner continues with 2♠ or 2NT. The 3◇ rebid is no longer forcing.

     ♠ A 2   ♡ Q J 7 4 2   ◇ K Q 8 6 4 3   ♣ - - -

Over 1♣, respond 1◇. You are strong enough to bid 1◇, then bid 2♡ and rebid 3♡, even if partner has not yet shown support.

TIPS 21-35: Competitive bidding

TIP 21:

When contemplating an overcall, apply the suit quality test to check whether the suit itself is adequate.

To make a suit overcall you should have a strong suit, so that it is a sound lead-directing bid and also minimises the risk of incurring penalties. It is rare to suffer a low-level penalty but if your overcalls are solid, penalties will be rarer still. It is almost always wrong to make an immediate overcall on a suit like J-x-x-x-x or 10-x-x-x-x-x.

How strong should a suit overcall be? At the 1-level, expect 8+ HCP, at the 2-level 10+ HCP and at the 3-level 12+ HCP. Another guide is to use losers: Maximum number of losers + level of bidding = 9, so that an overcall should have 8 losers or fewer at the 1-level, 7 losers or fewer at the 2-level and 6 losers or fewer at the 3-level. In addition, the suit should be able to pass the Suit Quality Test:

Length in Overcall Suit + Honours in the Overcall Suit should equal or exceed the number of tricks for which you are bidding. Thus, length + honours should be 7+ for a 1-level overcall, 8+ for a 2-level overcall and 9+ for a 3-level overcall. If the suit quality falls short by one, you should have maximum high card strength for the overcall. If the suit quality falls short by more than one, then you should pass or double or overcall 1NT, but do not overcall in your suit. You may pass and make a delayed overcall in your suit on the next round if the quality is inadequate for an immediate overcall.

In assessing the honours in your long suit, count the jack and ten as a full value only if supported by a higher honour.

SUIT	SUIT QUALITY	SUIT	SUIT QUALITY
J-x-x-x-x-x	6	K-Q-J-x	7
Q-x-x-x-x	6	Q-J-x-x-x	7
K-x-x-x-x	6	A-Q-x-x-x	7
A-x-x-x-x	6	A-x-x-x-x-x	7
A-K-x-x	6	Overcall in these suits at the	
Do not overcall in such suits.		1-level but not at the 2-level.	

SUIT	SUIT QUALITY	SUIT	SUIT QUALITY
A-K-J-x-x	8	A-K-Q-J-x	9
K-Q-J-x-x	8	K-Q-J-10-x	9
K-Q-x-x-x-x	8	A-K-J-x-x-x	9
Q-J-x-x-x-x	8	K-J-10-x-x-x	9

You may overcall in these suits at the 1-level or 2-level. Overcall in these suits at the 1-level or 2-level or 3-level.

Whether to double or overcall depends on the auction so far.

What should South do in these auctions?

SOUTH
♠ A K Q 8
♡ K 7
◇ J 8 7 4 3
♣ 6 2

(1)	WEST	NORTH	EAST	SOUTH
	1♣	No	1♡	?

(2)	WEST	NORTH	EAST	SOUTH
	1♣	No	1◇	?

(1) Your best action is to double as you have both unbid suits.

(2) Bid 1♠. This shows partner the best lead and may make it hard for E-W to find a heart fit. To double may attract a bid or lead in hearts.

What would you do with these cards if RHO opened 1♣, 1◇ or 1♠?

♠ Q 7 3   ♡ A J 6 3 2   ◇ K J   ♣ 6 5 4

Over 1♣ or 1◇, overcall 1♡. Over 1♠, you should pass. The heart suit is not good enough for a 2-level overcall, as the suit quality is 7.

What would you do with these cards if RHO opened 1♣, 1◇ or 1♡?

♠ J 8 6 4 3   ♡ A K 2   ◇ A 7 6   ♣ Q 5

Over 1♣, you can reasonably double. Over 1◇ or 1♡, you should pass, at least for the time being. The spade suit (quality = 5) is far too weak for an overcall. If LHO raises opener's suit to two and this comes back to you, a delayed 2♠ overcall is sensible. Your failure to overcall 1♠ marks you with a poor spade suit.

After (1♡) : No : (2♡), you should overcall 3♣ with:

♠ A 3   ♡ 7 4 2   ◇ 9 2   ♣ A K J 8 6 4

Suit quality = 9 and you have 12 HCP and 6½ losers.

TIP 22:

If partner opens 1NT and second hand intervenes, be prepared to bid 3NT with enough points for game and a no-trump hand type, even though you do not have a stopper in their suit.

Suppose partner opens 1NT and RHO bid 2♠, natural. What should you call with: ♠ 4 3 2   ♡ A 8 4   ◇ A Q J   ♣ Q 10 8 2?

Your best shot is 3NT, trusting partner to hold at least one spade stopper. This tip applies only if partner opened 1NT and follows logically from normal bidding strategy. The overcall will not be based on a solid suit like A-K-Q-x-x-x. With such a holding one would pass (or double) and defend against 1NT. A suit overcall over 1NT is normally based on a suit like A-Q-10-x-x-x, K-Q-10-9-x-x, K-J-10-x-x-x or similar with a suit quality of 8+.

Since the overcaller will not have a solid suit and you have no stopper in their suit, where will the missing high cards in their suit be? Almost always partner will have them, as you have enough strength for game.

Common agreements after an intervening bid over 1NT are:
* Change of suit below 3♡ is not forcing, e.g., 1NT : (2♠) : 3♣
* Jump-bids below game are forcing, e.g., 1NT : (2◇) : 3♠
* Bidding their suit = Stayman. 1NT : (2♠) : 3♠ shows four hearts.

Those who like to play transfers after 1NT can retain them after an overcall by using the highly effective Rubinsohl Convention:
* Suit bids at the 2-level are not forcing, e.g., 1NT : (2◇) : 2♠
* 2NT / 3♣ / 3◇ / 3♡ are transfers to the next suit along.
  Exception: Bidding the suit below the enemy suit = Stayman:
  1NT : (2♡) : 3◇ = Stayman, promises 4 spades. With 4 spades, opener can bid 3♠ strong, 4♠ weak. Without 4 spades, opener bids 3NT with a stopper in hearts and 3♡ with no stopper there.
  After a transfer, responder can show a second suit or show / deny a stopper: 1NT : (2♡) : 3♣ = transfer to diamonds. Over 3◇ by opener, responder can bid 3NT to show a heart stopper, 3♡ to deny one.
* 3♠ always shows no stopper in their suit, no 4-card major.
* 3NT always shows a stopper in their suit but no 4-card major.

TIP 23:

Do not commit yourself to 3NT until you have made sure a major suit game is not feasible.

Suppose partner opens 1♠. What would you respond with:

♠ Q 7　♡ A K 6 2　◇ A J 3　♣ J 10 8 2

It could be an error to bid 3NT at once. Start with 2♣ and if partner does not reveal a heart suit or 6+ spades, you can try 3NT then. You are better off in 4♡ opposite:　♠ K J 8 6 5　♡ Q 9 7 5　◇ 6　♣ A Q 3.

WEST	WEST	NORTH	EAST	SOUTH
♠ Q J 3		1◇	Dble	No
♡ K 7	?			
◇ Q 10 4 3				
♣ A Q 8 2	What action should West take?			

Many would choose 3NT but that would be premature. If partner has five spades, 4♠ may well be superior. Some possible continuations:

WEST	EAST	WEST	NORTH	EAST	SOUTH
♠ Q J 3	♠ A 9 5 4		1◇	Dble	No
♡ K 7	♡ A 8 6 2	2◇ (1)	No	2♡	No
◇ Q 10 4 3	◇ 6 2	3NT (2)	No	No	No
♣ A Q 8 2	♣ K J 5	(1) Artificial, forcing to suit agreement.			
		(2) As 2♡ denies holding five spades.			

WEST	EAST	WEST	NORTH	EAST	SOUTH
♠ Q J 3	♠ K 8 4 2		1◇	Dble	No
♡ K 7	♡ A J 6	2◇	No	2♠	No
◇ Q 10 4 3	◇ 6 2	2NT (1)	No	3NT	All pass
♣ A Q 8 2	♣ K J 9 7	(1) East could still have five spades for the			
		2♠ reply, so West marks time with 2NT.			

WEST	EAST	WEST	NORTH	EAST	SOUTH
♠ Q J 3	♠ K 8 6 5 2		1◇	Dble	No
♡ K 7	♡ A Q J 4	2◇	No	2♠	No
◇ Q 10 4 3	◇ 6	2NT	No	3♡ (1)	No
♣ A Q 8 2	♣ K 4 3	4♠	No	No	No
		(1) Four hearts and therefore five spades			

TIP 24:

Do not allow your opponents to play a suit part-score at the two-level unless you have length and strength in their suit. If the opponents hold a primary trump fit (they bid and raise a suit) it is almost always wrong to pass it out at the 2-level.

WEST
- ♠ A J 7 4 2
- ♡ K J 3
- ◇ 6
- ♣ K Q 8 2

West's rebid?

(1)	WEST	NORTH	EAST	SOUTH
	1♠	2◇	No	No
	?			

(2)	WEST	NORTH	EAST	SOUTH
	1♠	2♣	No	No
	?			

(1) Double to ask partner to choose spades, hearts or clubs (or perhaps to pass for penalties).

(2) Pass. You have length and strength in their suit.

Suppose the bidding has been:

WEST	NORTH	EAST	SOUTH
1♡	1♠	2♡	2♠
No	No	?	

East should invariably compete to the 3-level. When both sides have a trump fit and the points are roughly even, both sides can usually make eight tricks. Occasionally one side makes seven and the other makes nine. It pays to be consistent and always push to the 3-level in auctions such as these. The possibilities are:

• You make your 3-level contract. Obviously better than passing.

• You are one down in your 3-level contract. Better than passing if they would have made their contract, as they usually would.

• They push to the 3-level above you and fail. Again you are better off.

• They push to the 3-level above you and make. You are no worse off than if you had passed it out at the 2-level.

• You fail at the 3-level and it costs more than their contract was worth. This is feasible but rare. Even when vulnerable it pays you not to sell out at the 2-level. (Note also Tip 3 on part-score strategy.)

TIP 25:

If the opponents bid and raise a suit to the 2-level and then pass, be anxious to re-open the bidding in the pass-out seat with a delayed overcall, a delayed double or a delayed 2NT.

If the auction has been something like:

WEST	NORTH	EAST	SOUTH	WEST	NORTH	EAST	SOUTH
		1♡	No	1♣	No	1♡	No
2♡	No	No	?	2♡	No	No	?

It is usually wrong to pass the bidding out. The opponents have found a trump fit but have not tried for game. They do not have 25-26 points and probably not even 23-24 (one of them would have made a game try). Each side will have about half the points and if they have a trump fit, you probably have one, too. In that case, do not sell out at the 2-level: Tip 24. (This advice does not apply to rubber bridge if the 2-level contract would give the opponents game. In that case they may have considerable undisclosed strength.)

Actions available when you have not entered the bidding earlier:

• *The delayed overcall:* This is normally a 5+ suit. The suit will be poor if you could have overcalled it at the 1-level. In the above auctions:

South: ♠ 10 8 7 6 4 3   ♡ 8 7 3   ◇ A 8   ♣ K 7 — Bid 2♠.

South: ♠ 8   ♡ J 7 4 3   ◇ K Q 9 7 6 2   ♣ Q 2 — Bid 3◇.

• *The delayed double:* This shows support or tolerance for the unbid suits. South would double 2♡ with:

♠ K 8 6 4   ♡ 7   ◇ A 6 5 3   ♣ J 8 7 2

• *The delayed 2NT:* This shows support for both minors, at least four cards in each. South would bid 2NT over 2♡ with:

♠ 6 2   ♡ 5 3   ◇ K 9 8 4   ♣ A J 5 4 2

After partner's delayed action as above, keep the bidding at the cheapest level. Partner's failure to take action earlier signifies weakness and the delayed action already takes your strength into account.

TIP 26:

Do not compete to the 4-level with only part-score values.

In order to make $4\heartsuit$ or $4\spadesuit$ you require 25-26 points. To make $4\clubsuit$ or $4\diamondsuit$ you logically need the same. If both sides are in the auction and you know you do not have the values for game, it is unwise to venture beyond the 3-level. When the points are roughly even and both sides have a trump fit both sides can usually make eight tricks, occasionally one side can make nine tricks but it is rare for either side to make ten tricks. If one assumes the success rate for a 4-level venture is about 1-in-4 (possibly lower), you need to be right at least 4 times out of 5 to show even a slight profit.

Often you will go minus when they were going minus at the 3-level. Do not assume the opponents are infallible. They are prone to error and may well fail at the 3-level. Why take that result away from them?

There is also a far higher incidence of penalty doubles at the 4-level since they know you are bidding beyond your means. While you frequently escape unscathed with your 2-level and 3-level competitive manoeuvres, this invulnerability does not extend to the 4-level.

NORTH	WEST	NORTH	EAST	SOUTH
$\spadesuit$ 8 7 3	1$\spadesuit$	No	2$\spadesuit$	Double
$\heartsuit$ 9 2	3$\spadesuit$	?		
$\diamondsuit$ J 3				
$\clubsuit$ K Q 10 7 6 5	What action should North take?			

Answer: Do not compete for a part-score at the 4-level. Pass and lead the $\clubsuit$K if the bidding ends here. If partner is very strong, partner will take further action, perhaps doubling again for takeout.

NORTH	WEST	NORTH	EAST	SOUTH
$\spadesuit$ A 3	1$\clubsuit$	No	1$\heartsuit$	No
$\heartsuit$ 7 6	2$\heartsuit$	No	No	3$\diamondsuit$
$\diamondsuit$ Q 8 5 4	3$\heartsuit$	?		
$\clubsuit$ K 7 6 4 2	What action should North take?			

Answer: Pass. Partner's delayed 3$\diamondsuit$ has already pushed them one higher.

TIP 27:

If an opponent passes after long consideration, you should probably pass, too.

If the bidding has started:

WEST	NORTH	EAST	SOUTH
1♠	No	2♠	No
No	?		

Tips 24 and 25 recommended that you dislodge the opponents from the 2-level – do not sell out at two if they have a trump fit – and find some delayed action to push them to the 3-level. The essence of successful part-score bidding is to push them from the safety of the 2-level to the jeopardy of the 3-level.

However, if West thought for a long time before passing 2♠, North should pass out 2♠ unless action is clear-cut. The reason for the long trance is obvious: West was very close to inviting game. If you give the opponents another chance, the auction may develop like this:

WEST	NORTH	EAST	SOUTH
1♠	No	2♠	No
No*	Dble	3♠	No
4♠	No	No	No

*After much deliberation

East, picking up the message from West's trance, pushes to 3♠ and West bids one more. Now you have to defend a touch-and-go game. If the cards lie luckily for them, 4♠ might make. It is most annoying to chalk up a game to them when you could have passed it out at two. Save yourself the anguish and let sleeping dogs lie.

It is true that the Laws state that East must not be influenced by partner's hesitation, but you are better off protecting yourself than having a confrontation with East, who will claim 'I was super-maximum for my raise . . . did partner really hesitate? . . . I did not even notice', and so on. Even if you do pursue it, there is no guarantee that an Appeals Committee will see it your way. Look after yourself rather than bleat later, 'We wuz robbed'.

TIP 28:

To assist partner in determining the combined trump length, it is sensible to use 'support doubles' by opener.

Suppose the bidding starts this way:

WEST	NORTH	EAST	SOUTH
1 ◇	No	1 ♠	2 ♣
?			

What should West do with:

(1) ♠ K 8 5   (2) ♠ K 8 5 4   (3) ♠ Q 6
      ♡ 8 4   ♡ 8 4   ♡ 8 4 2
      ◇ A K 7 4 3 2   ◇ A K 7 4 2   ◇ A K 7 4 3 2
      ♣ K 2   ♣ K 2   ♣ K 2

If opener bids 2 ◇ with (1), a spade fit may go begging. If opener bids 2 ♠ with (1) and (2), how will partner know the degree of support?

To solve such problems, many partnerships use a double in this situation to guarantee 3-card support for responder's major. This use is known as a 'support double'. The principle: If responder bids a major and next player intervenes at the 1-level or 2-level, a raise by opener shows 4-card support and double shows precisely 3-card support. On that basis:

(1) Double. Shows 3 spades. It is ambiguous about strength or about the length in diamonds. Opener could have a powerful hand, enough to invite game or insist on game.

(2) Bid 2 ♠. When playing support doubles, this guarantees 4-card support. Then if the opponents compete to 3 ♡, responder is well-placed to judge whether to bid 3 ♠ or pass.

(3) Bid 2 ◇. Not only does this show diamond length but when playing support doubles it also denies 3-card support. That means responder need not bother rebidding a 5-card suit.

If the bidding starts 1 ♣ : (No) : 1 ◇ : (1 ♠), double by opener here shows 4 hearts. The degree of support for diamonds is undisclosed.

TIP 29:

If you know your side has at least ten trumps, compete to game level. The weaker your hand, the more important it is to bid to game quickly, whether or not the opponents have bid.

You hold, as East:

♠ J 8 6 4 3   ♡ J 10 7 3 2   ◇ 6   ♣ 8 2

What would you do after this beginning?

WEST	NORTH	EAST	SOUTH
1♠	No	?	

If you play 5-card majors, you should jump to 4♠. Tip 10 is also relevant for East here. Playing 4-card suits it is not as clear but as opener will have 5+ spades more often than not, it is still a good pre-emptive move to bid 4♠. Let them try to find the best spot after that.

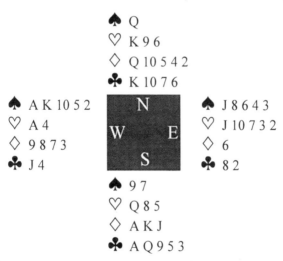

```
              ♠ Q
              ♡ K 9 6
              ◇ Q 10 5 4 2
              ♣ K 10 7 6
♠ A K 10 5 2           ♠ J 8 6 4 3
♡ A 4           N      ♡ J 10 7 3 2
◇ 9 8 7 3    W     E   ◇ 6
♣ J 4           S      ♣ 8 2
              ♠ 9 7
              ♡ Q 8 5
              ◇ A K J
              ♣ A Q 9 5 3
```

4♠ is one down. They can make 5♣ or 5◇. Will they be able to find it after 1♠ : (No) : 4♠?

East should find the same jump to 4♠ if North had taken action, such as double or an overcall.

TIP 30:

To maximize your competitive advantage after partner overcalls, it is sensible to play jump-raises of overcalls as pre-emptive.

Just as it is sound strategy to jump to game when you have a 10-card fit, so you should be prepared to compete for nine tricks when you know you have a 9-card fit. The weaker your hand, the quicker you should bid to the appropriate level.

WEST	NORTH	EAST	SOUTH
1♢	1♠	No	?

What should South do with each of these hands?

(1) ♠ Q J 3
♡ A 7 5 2
♢ J 6
♣ 9 8 4 2

(2) ♠ Q 8 7 4
♡ 9 8 7 2
♢ J
♣ Q J 5 2

(3) ♠ Q 8 4
♡ 9 8
♢ A K 3 2
♣ Q 9 4 2

(4) ♠ Q 8 7 4
♡ Q 8
♢ A K 3
♣ K 9 4 2

(5) ♠ Q 8 7 4 2
♡ 8
♢ 10 6 5 3 2
♣ K J

(6) ♠ Q 8 7 4 2
♡ A K 4
♢ 10 6
♣ A Q J

(1) Bid 2♠. Normal single raise.

(2) Jump to 3♠, a pre-emptive raise. Expectancy for this bid is about 8 losers, 4-card support and below 10 HCP. Partner should almost always pass this weak raise.

(3) Start with 2♢, showing a strong hand. If partner rebids 2♠ to show a minimum overcall, pass. Over 2♡, 2♠ by you is enough.

(4) Start with 2♢ but if partner bids 2♠, you are worth one more effort with 3♠. Some play that a jump to 3♢ shows 4-card support for the overcall and around 13-15 HCP with 7 losers.

(5) Jump to 4♠ (Tip 29).

(6) Start with 2♢ and bid 4♠ on the next round. This shows a hand with enough high card strength for game and good defensive values.

TIP 31:

When considering a penalty double of a suit below game, you need strength and length in their suit. The Rule of 10 & 12 indicates the minimum requirements for your holding in the enemy suit if the double is to be profitable.

The most rewarding penalties can occur at the 1-level, 2-level or 3-level if you have the right requirements:

(1) Strength and length in their suit.

(2) 20+ HCP between you and partner.

(3) A misfit with partner's suit.

The Rule of 10 & 12:

(i) Add your expected trump tricks to the number of tricks the opponents are trying to win. For a good double, the answer should be 10 or more. If below 10, the double is unsound.

(ii) Add the number of trumps you hold to the number of tricks the opponents are trying to win. If the answer is 12 or more, you have adequate trump length. If below 12, the double is unsound.

Part (i) measures the trump strength needed:

Doubles at the 1-level: $10 - 7$ tricks = 3 trump winners needed.
Doubles at the 2-level: $10 - 8$ tricks = 2 trump winners needed.
Doubles at the 3-level: $10 - 9$ tricks = 1 trump winner needed.

How do you assess winners in their suit? Assume declarer leads the suit from the top and estimate how many tricks that will give you. These are not sure tricks but potential winners. For example:

Q-10-8-5-3: Estimate three tricks. If declarer starts with ace and king, you have Q-10-8 left against declarer's presumed J-9-7.

K-Q-9-6: Estimate three tricks. After ace and jack, which you win, you have K-9 left against declarer's presumed 10.

K-Q-7-6: Estimate two tricks. After the ace and jack, which you win, declarer's 10-9 against your K-7 gives you just one more trick.

♠ 7   Partner opens 1♠. Next player overcalls.
♡ Q 10 3   Would you contemplate playing for penalties
♢ A J 8 6 3   if RHO bid:
♣ K 9 5 2   (a) 2♣?   (b) 2♢?   (c) 2♡?

(a) Do not consider penalties. You have only one potential club trick. $1 + 8 = 9$, short of the 10 needed for penalties.

(b) Definitely aim for penalties. You have three potential diamond tricks: $3 + 8 = 11$, more than the required total of 10. In addition your side has more than 20 HCP and you have a misfit with partner.

If double by you here would be for penalties, double. If playing negative doubles (for takeout), pass and then pass again if partner produces the expected re-opening takeout double. Opener is expected to re-open with a takeout double if short in their suit. With the penalties hand, you will pass. With a weak hand, you will answer the double.

(c) Do not look for penalties. You have only one potential trump trick.

Part (ii) measures whether you have sufficient length in their suit:

Doubles at the 1-level: $12 - 7$ tricks = 5 trumps needed.
Doubles at the 2-level: $12 - 8$ tricks = 4 trumps needed.
Doubles at the 3-level: $12 - 9$ tricks = 3 trumps needed.

It follows that—

To play for penalties at the 1-level, you need at least five trumps, including three tricks in the trump suit.

To play for penalties at the 2-level, you need at least four trumps, including two tricks in the trump suit.

To play for penalties at the 3-level, you need at least three trumps, including one trick in the trump suit.

It pays to be conservative at the 1-level. If you can defeat them, you are making a contract of at least one with a known bad trump split. If sitting over declarer, a minimum trump holding might be K-Q-10-x-x. If sitting under declarer, you should be stronger, with a suggested minimum of K-Q-J-9-x.

Dealer West : Both vulnerable

West	North	East	South
1♠	Dble	Rdble	2♣
?			

East's redouble shows 10+ HCP and an interest in penalties. Double by West would be for penalties here. Should West double with:

♠ A 10 9 7 5 2   ♡ A 6   ◇ 7 2   ♣ K J 4

Applying Part (i), you have two expected trump tricks and they are bidding for eight tricks. 8 + 2 = 10. Your holding satisfies Part (i).

You have only three trumps. 3 + 8 = 11, less than the 12 needed to satisfy Part (ii) about trump length.

West should therefore pass and let partner clarify the redouble. In a national selection tournament, West did double in the above situation. This was the deal:

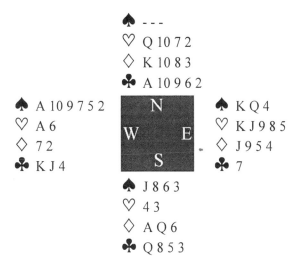

With support for spades, East should not have started with a redouble or should have removed the double (4♠ made in the other room), but East clearly expected better clubs from West. Declarer was not really tested and 2♣ doubled made with an overtrick.

TIP 32:

Be very wary of playing for penalties at a low level, even if you have five good trumps, if partner is known to be void in trumps.

1.   Dealer East : Both vulnerable

West	North	East	South
		1♣	1♠
No	2♠	Dble (1)	No
?			

(1) For takeout

What action would you take as West with:

♠ K Q 7 5 4   ♡ J   ◇ K 6 5 4   ♣ J 7 4

2.   Dealer West : North-South vulnerable

West	North	East	South
1♡	Dble	Rdble	3♣
No	No	?	

What action would you take as East with:

♠ Q 8 6 2   ♡ J 5   ◇ 9 7 5   ♣ A K 10 8

Do you agree with the redouble?

Solution to 1:

The temptation is to pass for penalties, but you should consider two factors. Given your spade holding, South almost certainly has five spades and North will have three. That means partner will be void and will be unable to lead a trump through declarer.

In addition, it means partner will have 5+ clubs (if 1-4-4-4, East would open 1◇) and declarer or dummy might be short in clubs. Partner's high cards in clubs may not translate into tricks. One of the features for sound low-level penalties is a misfit with partner (Tip 31). That does not exist here.

If you choose not to pass for penalties, the obvious bid is 3◇. There is nothing wrong with electing to defend as long as you defeat the contract.

The deal arose in a 2002 national pairs event, with Imp scoring.

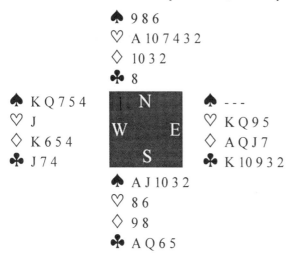

♠ 9 8 6
♡ A 10 7 4 3 2
♢ 10 3 2
♣ 8

♠ K Q 7 5 4
♡ J
♢ K 6 5 4
♣ J 7 4

♠ - - -
♡ K Q 9 5
♢ A Q J 7
♣ K 10 9 3 2

♠ A J 10 3 2
♡ 8 6
♢ 9 8
♣ A Q 6 5

West passed the double and led the ♡J, taken by the ace. Declarer finessed the ♣Q, cashed the ♣A and ruffed a club, leaving:

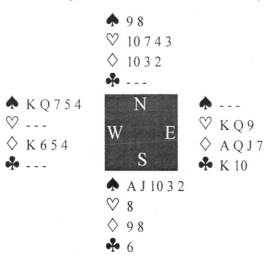

♠ 9 8
♡ 10 7 4 3
♢ 10 3 2
♣ - - -

♠ K Q 7 5 4
♡ - - -
♢ K 6 5 4
♣ - - -

♠ - - -
♡ K Q 9
♢ A Q J 7
♣ K 10

♠ A J 10 3 2
♡ 8
♢ 9 8
♣ 6

A diamond from dummy saw East play the ♢J. While there are a number of ways to defeat the contract, the defence slipped and allowed declarer to ruff a diamond cheaply, –670. Bidding 3♢ would have been better.

Solution to 2:

The deal arose in the final of a 2002 national teams championship:

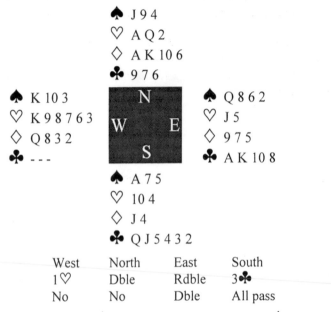

♠ J 9 4
♥ A Q 2
♦ A K 10 6
♣ 9 7 6

♠ K 10 3　　　　　　　♠ Q 8 6 2
♥ K 9 8 7 6 3　　　　♥ J 5
♦ Q 8 3 2　　　　　　 ♦ 9 7 5
♣ - - -　　　　　　　　♣ A K 10 8

♠ A 7 5
♥ 10 4
♦ J 4
♣ Q J 5 4 3 2

West	North	East	South
1♥	Dble	Rdble	3♣
No	No	Dble	All pass

Declarer ducked the ♦8 lead to the jack, finessed the ♦10 and ditched two spades on the ♦A and ♦K, as East discarded the ♥5. Ten tricks were made for +870, +14 Imps as 3NT N-S failed at the other table.

Although West had a featherweight opening, this was not the prime cause of the disaster. West could have a robust 12-count and 3♣ doubled might still make. Perhaps West should have bid over 3♣.

As redouble suggests not just 10+ HCP but also a misfit with partner and the ability to double at least two suits for penalties, a 1NT response (or even 1♠) is better. Passing 3♣ is not an option, as the redouble promises another bid. In fact, the redouble end-played East in the bidding.

The double of 3♣ was at best a trifle naive. South had heard the redouble and nevertheless had jumped to 3♣ at unfavourable vulnerability. Unless South has death wish, East should be able to predict the likely club layout and that West would be void. That in turn argues against playing for penalties at this level.

TIP 33:

Do not double an artificial cue-bid or an artificial bid in a relay system sequence without a very good reason.

When their side clearly has the balance of strength and they embark on a cue-bidding sequence, there is a constant temptation to double a cue-bid with some strength in that suit in order to indicate a good lead to partner. You should almost always resist that desire unless you feel that only that lead from partner will defeat their slam.

The reasons against speculative lead-directing doubles are:

1. If you are strong enough to believe the slam is likely to fail anyway, your double may inhibit them from reaching the failing slam.

2. By revealing where your strength lies, you allow the opponents to upgrade the value of a singleton holding in that suit and thus reach a slam they might otherwise have avoided.

3. If they have reached cue-bids of second-round controls and you double a cue-bid of the king when you hold A-Q, you may drive them into a making slam, such as 6NT, from the right side rather than a possibly failing slam, when partner finds the lead without your double.

4. Doubles in a cue-bidding auction give the opponents extra space to exchange information. For example:

West	North	East	South
1♠	No	3♠	No
4♣	No	4♦	Double . . .

West can redouble to show second-round control or to pass to deny it. If West passes, East can redouble to show second-round control or bid anything else without such control. Without South's double, East-West would be much higher before this information could be exchanged.

Likewise, modern relay systems function best with plenty of bidding space. A double in a relay auction gives them more space, as it allows two additional actions (pass and redouble). This saves two steps and gives the relayers more room to move. This is an expensive price if the double is not essential.

TIP 34:

Do not sacrifice on flat hands.

Dealer South : Nil vulnerable

West	North	East	South
			3♣
No	?		

What action would you take as North with:

♠ 8 6 4   ♡ 7 6 3   ◇ K 5 4   ♣ Q 7 6 2

What would your answer be if West had doubled 3♣ for takeout?

It is tempting to jump to 5♣ since the opponents are clearly cold for a game. Nevertheless, it is better not to bid 5♣ in either case. If 5♣ is doubled the cost will certainly be more than their game is worth. That is a common consequence of sacrificing with a flat hand.

For a non-vulnerable pre-empt, expectancy is six tricks. You bring two tricks, the ◇K and ♣Q. That brings the tally to eight tricks and so 5♣ doubled will usually be three down, –500, too much at this vulnerability. If the ◇K turns out not to be a trick, the cost can be –800.

The deal might look like this:

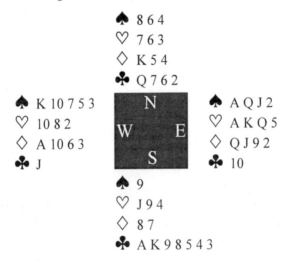

```
                  ♠ 8 6 4
                  ♡ 7 6 3
                  ◇ K 5 4
                  ♣ Q 7 6 2
 ♠ K 10 7 5 3         N          ♠ A Q J 2
 ♡ 10 8 2                        ♡ A K Q 5
 ◇ A 10 6 3     W         E      ◇ Q J 9 2
 ♣ J                 S          ♣ 10
                  ♠ 9
                  ♡ J 9 4
                  ◇ 8 7
                  ♣ A K 9 8 5 4 3
```

West	North	East	South
			3♣
No	5♣	Dble	No
?			

If North bids 5♣, East will double and West cannot get it wrong. A 5♠ contract will make and passing 5♣ doubled scores +500.

It is reasonable for North to pass 3♣, but the best shot after 3♣ : (No) is a subtle 4♣. One advantage is that East's double may be less clearly for takeout and –300 would be a good result, whether you are playing pairs or teams or rubber bridge.

Another drawback to jumping to 5♣ is that you tip them off that you have a big fit in clubs. This may push them into a making slam they might otherwise not have bid. *Give partner's pre-empt a chance to work.*

Suppose that they do have slam available (simply switch the East-West diamonds and they can make 6♠). If you pass 3♣, East will double for takeout and West might jump to 4♠. This could fire East into trying for the slam, which will succeed.

Again it may work better for you to bid 4♣ after West passes. If the bidding starts 3♣ : (No) : 4♣ : (Double), West will certainly bid just 4♠, not 5♠. East will now have no reason to look for a slam since the 4♠ reply does not promise any significant values.

Suppose the East-West hands opposite are interchanged. Now the bidding would start 3♣ : (Double). Here, too, North should either pass or bid 4♣. If you jump to 5♣ and that is doubled, the cost now would be –800. East-West do have a slam available and if the auction bounces 3♣ : (Double) : 5♣ : (5♠), West is likely to raise to 6♠. Whether you pass 3♣ or bid 4♣, they may still bid the slam but at least you have not pushed them into it.

Bidding 4♣ over the double is still attractive. It may not help on this deal, since East would bid 4♠ over 4♣ and they might well bid 6♠ now. Still, bidding 4♣ prevents East's using it as a cue-bid to show a two-suited hand, particularly one with both majors.

TIP 35:

Do not double a suit slam with just two aces or with just very strong trumps.

Suppose the bidding has been:

West	North	East	South
1♥	No	3♣	No
3♥	No	6♥	No
No	?		

With which of these hands should North double?

(a) ♠ A J 7 3   (b) ♠ K 5 3
    ♥ 7 2   ♥ Q J 10 9
    ♦ A 8 7 6 2   ♦ 8 7
    ♣ 6 2   ♣ 9 6 3 2

The answer is the same for both hands. North should not double in either case. For (a), unless the opponents are the rawest beginners, they will have heard of Blackwood and would not jump to slam missing two aces without checking first. Why did they not ask for aces? Because they are not concerned about two aces missing. Why not? Because East is staring at a void. For example:

WEST	EAST
♠ K Q 8	♠ - - -
♥ K J 10 6 4 3	♥ A Q 9 5
♦ Q J 9	♦ K 10 3
♣ 8	♣ A K 9 7 5 4

If North does double with hand (a), it would be no surprise if East redoubled. Thus North is risking to lose an extra 640 (6♥ = 180 vs 6♥ redoubled for 720 + 100 for the insult) to gain an extra 50 points (or 100 if East-West are vulnerable). North would need to be right 13 times out of 14 (or 7 out of 8 if East-West are vulnerable) just to start showing a tiny profit. Clearly there is no percentage in doubling a slam just because you have two aces. If the slam fails, you have an excellent result anyway. You do not need to double to improve on that.

Corollary: If you have a void and intend to bid slam anyway, you may as well ask for aces or key cards with 4NT.

By using 4NT you are not telegraphing your void to the opponents. As ace leads are more popular against slams than they deserve to be, you may find an opponent leads the ace of the suit in which you are void. This might set up useful winners for you in the other hand. If you jump to slam without asking for aces / key cards, an opponent will be reluctant to lead an ace because of the risk of its being ruffed.

With hand (b) you are certain of defeating 6♡ but that is the only slam you can beat for sure. It would be dumb to double 6♡ and find them running to 6NT which you cannot beat. For example:

WEST	EAST
♠ A J 6	♠ Q 4 2
♡ A 8 6 5 3 2	♡ K 7 4
◇ K Q J	◇ A 9
♣ 8	♣ A K Q J 5

East-West are unlucky to reach 6♡, which fails on the 4-0 break. 6NT is superior, since it may succeed when hearts behave or as long as clubs are not 5-2 or worse if the hearts split badly.

If North does double 6♡ when holding ♡Q-J-10-9, either East or West may sniff out the problem and run to 6NT. That would give North-South a terrible result instead of a great one. The loss would be over 1000 points (–990 / –1440 vs +50 / +100).

The moral is that if the opponents have reached a slam which is due to fail, you do not need to double to obtain a good score. Not at rubber bridge, not at match-pointed pairs, not at teams. Furthermore, if you regularly refrain from doubling their slams with holdings like K-Q-J, Q-J-10-9 or J-10-9-8-x of trumps, you will gain a solid reputation for having a generous and magnanimous nature.

TIPS 36-55: Opening leads

TIP 36:

In general it pays to lead a suit bid by partner, even though the opponents have bid no-trumps afterwards.

Suppose the bidding has been: What should West lead from:

WEST	NORTH	EAST	SOUTH
	1♦	1♡	1NT
No	3NT	All pass	

(a) ♠ J 10 7 3 2 (b) ♠ J 10 7 3 2
    ♡ 8 2   ♡ 8 2
    ♦ Q 4   ♦ A K
    ♣ 6 5 4 3   ♣ 6 5 4 3

An opening bid may be made on a weak suit, but an overcall includes a strong lead-directing suggestion. While it is normal to lead partner's overcalled suit, many players strike out elsewhere when partner's overcall is followed by a no-trump bid, showing at least one stopper in partner's suit. This strategy is short-sighted. Yes, they do have a stopper, but your function is to eliminate that stopper. If you do not lead partner's suit, they will still have that stopper. For example:

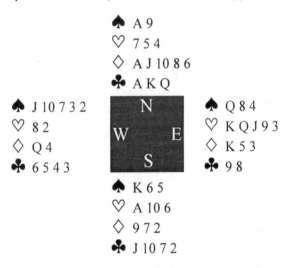

♠ A 9
♡ 7 5 4
♦ A J 10 8 6
♣ A K Q

♠ J 10 7 3 2   ♠ Q 8 4
♡ 8 2   ♡ K Q J 9 3
♦ Q 4   ♦ K 5 3
♣ 6 5 4 3   ♣ 9 8

♠ K 6 5
♡ A 10 6
♦ 9 7 2
♣ J 10 7 2

A heart lead will defeat 3NT. On any other lead declarer has ten tricks.

If partner has a suit like K-Q-J-10-x or A-Q-J-10-x, declarer will have one stopper. Your lead eliminates that stopper and sets up the rest of the suit as winners. If partner's suit is something like K-J-10-x-x or K-Q-10-x-x, declarer may have two stoppers with A-Q-x / A-J-x. Two leads of the suit are needed to knock out those stoppers, but if you decline to lead partner's good suit, those stoppers will still be there.

When should you lead a suit other than partner's after such an auction? If you have a goodish 5+ suit *and entries*, then you may choose to lead your own suit. Even if your suit is strong, it will be of little avail if you have no entry later to your established winners.

With hand (b) a spade lead is a sound alternative to the heart, because of your diamond holding. Just as declarer, with a choice of suits to attack, would choose the long suit in the hand which has the entries, so the defenders must follow the same policy. For example:

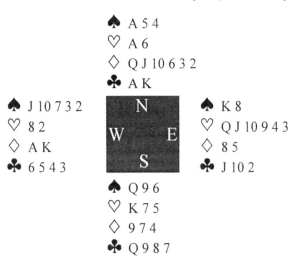

After the above auction, declarer could and almost certainly would succeed on a heart lead as East has no quick entry later. On a low spade lead, declarer is virtually certain to play low in dummy. East will win and as long as a spade comes back, 3NT can be defeated. Even if declarer rises with the ♠A at trick 1, East can defeat the game by a spectacular unblock of the ♠K.

TIP 37:

If you are leading partner's suit in which you hold three cards—
(1) Lead top from two touching cards headed by an honour
(2) Lead middle with no honour card in the suit
(3) Lead lowest from one honour, or two honours not touching

When partner bids a suit it is normal to lead that suit. The card to lead is the standard one from the given holding and not an abnormal one.

(1) From A-K-x, K-Q-x, Q-J-x, J-10-x, 10-9-x lead the top card.

(2) From three rag cards, some lead middle (and follow with the top card – middle-up-down or M.U.D.) while others lead the bottom card. The purpose is to deny a doubleton. With a doubleton, the order is higher-then-lower. With either of the above methods, partner will see lower-then-higher and can deduce therefore that your lead was not a doubleton. Therefore you hold at least one more card in the suit. This information can be essential for a defender.

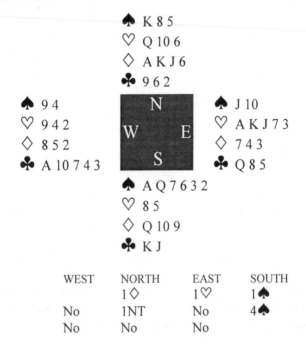

```
                    ♠ K 8 5
                    ♡ Q 10 6
                    ◇ A K J 6
                    ♣ 9 6 2
   ♠ 9 4              N          ♠ J 10
   ♡ 9 4 2                       ♡ A K J 7 3
   ◇ 8 5 2        W     E        ◇ 7 4 3
   ♣ A 10 7 4 3      S           ♣ Q 8 5
                    ♠ A Q 7 6 3 2
                    ♡ 8 5
                    ◇ Q 10 9
                    ♣ K J
```

WEST	NORTH	EAST	SOUTH
	1◇	1♡	1♠
No	1NT	No	4♠
No	No	No	

If West leads the *nine* of hearts, East may try to cash three rounds of hearts, reading West's high-then-low as a doubleton and placing South with three hearts. If West leads low-then-high, East can deduce, after the second round of hearts, that South will ruff the third round. With no hope of more tricks in the red suits, East should switch to a club.

Best is the ♣5, bottom from honour to three. If South plays the king, the defence can take two clubs and beat 4♠. If South plays the jack, 4♠ makes. Without a club switch from East by trick 3, the defence has no chance. If East plays a third heart, South ruffs, draws trumps and discards a club on the thirteenth diamond.

Top-of-nothing (leading the highest card when no honour is held) is less risky in no-trumps but it may still mislead partner as to the length held by you and hence by declarer. Consider this layout in no-trumps:

$$\heartsuit 7\ 6$$
$$\heartsuit 9\ 4\ 2 \qquad \heartsuit A\ K\ J\ 5\ 3$$
$$\heartsuit Q\ 10\ 8$$

If West leads the ♡9, East may place South with ♡Q-10-x-x and may win the first lead and switch instead of setting up the suit.

It is safe to lead top-of-nothing when partner knows you cannot hold a doubleton. Suppose the bidding for the above layout had started:

WEST	NORTH	EAST	SOUTH
		1♡	No
2♡	Dble	No	2NT . . .

Now it is sensible to lead the ♡9 denying an honour, as West is bound to have at least three cards for the raise.

(3) From three to an honour, such as K-7-2, Q-8-3, J-6-5, 10-4-2, the standard lead is the bottom card. To lead the top card can cost. Witness:

(a)   A 5
     K 7 2   Q 9 8 4 3
          J 10 6

Lead the king and South has two tricks. Lead low and South has only one.

(b)   10 2
     Q 8 3   A 9 7 6 5
          K J 4

Lead the queen and South has two tricks. Lead low and South can be held to one trick.

(c)
      8 5
  A 4 3   K J 10 9 2
      Q 7 6

Lead the ace and South makes a trick. Lead low and East can win with the king and return the jack. South makes no tricks.

(d)
      A 2
  J 7 5   Q 9 8 6 4
      K 10 3

Lead the jack and South can make three tricks (win the ace and later finesse the ten). Lead low and South can be held to two tricks.

From A-x-x, lead low against no-trumps but if you must lead from this holding against a suit contract, start with the ace.

Not only may the top card from honour-third cost a trick, it may also destroy a complete defence. For example:

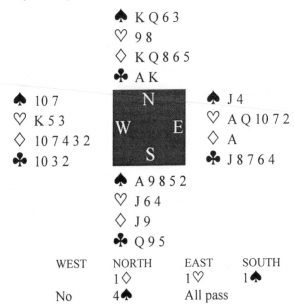

♠ K Q 6 3
♡ 9 8
♢ K Q 8 6 5
♣ A K

♠ 10 7   ♠ J 4
♡ K 5 3   ♡ A Q 10 7 2
♢ 10 7 4 3 2   ♢ A
♣ 10 3 2   ♣ J 8 7 6 4

♠ A 9 8 5 2
♡ J 6 4
♢ J 9
♣ Q 9 5

WEST	NORTH	EAST	SOUTH
	1♢	1♡	1♠
No	4♠	All pass	

If West leads the ♡K, South has no problems making 4♠. On the correct lead of the *three* of hearts, East wins with the ♡A and plays off the ♢A to create the void. East returns a low heart to West's king (needed as an entry) and ruffs the diamond return for one down.

Moral: It is unsound to play top of partner's suit automatically.

62

TIP 38:

When making a short suit lead in no-trumps, prefer an unbid major to an unbid minor.

Situations where you might prefer a short suit lead in no-trumps:

- Your opponents have shown length in your long suit.

- Your long suit is hopelessly weak and your hand has no entries.

- Your long suit is an unattractive 4-card suit.

WEST
♠ 8 4 3
♥ A J 6 4 2
♦ 9 5 2
♣ A 2

What should West lead after this auction?

WEST	NORTH	EAST	SOUTH
		No	1♥
No	2♣	No	2NT
No	3NT	All pass	

Without South's 1♥ bid, a low heart would appeal. It is unwise to lead into the opening bidder's suit unless you have a 4-card or longer sequence, such as Q-J-10-9-x. With hearts and clubs excluded, it is a guess between spades and diamonds, but a spade lead stands a better chance. As opponents are likely to bid any major suit they hold, the absence of a spade bid suggests that partner might have spade length. Opponents are less concerned about concealing a minor so that the absence of a diamond bid does not preclude their having length there.

WEST
♠ A J 4 2
♥ J 10 3
♦ J 10 3
♣ J 4 2

What should West lead after this auction?

WEST	NORTH	EAST	SOUTH
	No	No	1NT
No	No	No	

It is not attractive to lead from a 4-card suit with broken honours, such as A-Q-x-x or A-J-x-x, particularly against a 1NT contract, or where declarer opens 2NT passed out, or after 1NT : 2NT, passed out. Such leads are more likely to cost than to gain. A lead from a decent 3-card holding often works out better. Start with the ♥J (choose the major rather than the minor).

TIP 39:

If you have decided not to lead your long suit in no-trumps and hope to hit partner's length, beware of leading a major which partner could have conveniently indicated at the 1-level.

WEST
♠ 8 7 2
♡ J 6 5 3 2
♢ J 2
♣ 8 7 2

What should West lead after this auction?

WEST	NORTH	EAST	SOUTH
	1♡	No	1NT
No	3NT	All pass	

Following Tip 38 (lead a major rather than a minor when making a short suit lead), you might choose a spade here. There are clues to suggest a spade is not best. As you are so weak, partner probably has enough to bid, yet partner passed. The failure to overcall or double indicates partner does not have spade length. In that case, try a minor and lead a club (prefer the longer to the shorter). The full deal:

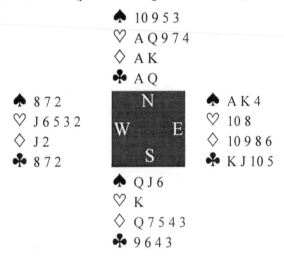

```
              ♠ 10 9 5 3
              ♡ A Q 9 7 4
              ♢ A K
              ♣ A Q
♠ 8 7 2          N          ♠ A K 4
♡ J 6 5 3 2   W     E       ♡ 10 8
♢ J 2            S          ♢ 10 9 8 6
♣ 8 7 2                     ♣ K J 10 5
              ♠ Q J 6
              ♡ K
              ♢ Q 7 5 4 3
              ♣ 9 6 4 3
```

The spade lead helps declarer set up the extra tricks needed while either red suit gives declarer time to unblock the diamonds and lead a spade, again establishing the tricks needed. A club lead sets up five tricks for the defence quickly. On other layouts a diamond lead might be best but East's silence means a spade lead is unlikely to work.

TIP 40:

Do not lead a suit bid or implied by the opposition.

Whether the contract is no-trumps or trumps, it is rarely worthwhile to lead a suit in which an opponent has length unless you have a solid 4+ sequence, such as K-Q-J-10-x or Q-J-10-9-x. Declarer will almost always have to tackle the long suit anyway to develop extra tricks. If you lead the suit, you are assisting declarer in that task.

Suppose they have bid, without interference, $1\heartsuit$: $2\clubsuit$, $2\heartsuit$: $4\heartsuit$. With no attractive lead, an average player might start with a club, especially from a doubleton. Some would try to justify this by referring to the 'lead-through-strength' rule. With a singleton club and a weak hand, a club lead might be reasonable but otherwise West should choose a spade or a diamond. The 'lead-through-strength' rule does *not* apply to the opening lead *and does not apply to a long suit in dummy.* Once dummy has appeared, usually apply the 'lead-through-strength' rule only to a doubleton or tripleton suit in dummy.

WEST

♠ Q 8 7 4 2
♡ A 2
◇ 7
♣ Q 8 7 4 2

What should West lead after this auction?

WEST	NORTH	EAST	SOUTH
		No	1NT
No	2♣	No	2♡
No	3NT	All pass	

On the basis of lead a major rather than a minor, you might choose a spade lead but that is a not logical move here. If the opponents had bid $1\heartsuit$: $1\spadesuit$, 1NT : 3NT you would not lead a spade. The above auction is the same in effect, South has shown hearts and North's use of Stayman followed by 3NT implies four spades. Reject the spade and try a club lead.

Similar logic applies if the opponents have bid $1\diamondsuit$: 1NT, passed out. You should be very wary of leading a club. Responder would have bid $1\heartsuit$ or $1\spadesuit$ with a 4+ suit and raised diamonds with 4+ support. It follows that declarer should have 4+ clubs and only a strong sequence would make a club lead attractive. Without that, choose your longer major or the stronger suit if they are of equal length.

TIP 41:

Pay close attention to the bidding. Inferences abound which may guide you to avoid foolish leads. Note the rule of suit length parity.

Whether the opponents alone are bidding or whether the auction is competitive there is much to be gleaned from the information revealed. The methods below may not be part of your system but you will have sequences where similar inferences can be applied.

WEST What should West lead after this auction?

♠ 6
Dealer East : Nil vulnerable

WEST	NORTH	EAST	SOUTH
♥ Q J 8 6 4 2		1♣ (1)	1♠
◇ K 5			
♣ J 7 6 3	2♥ (2) 2♠	3♥	3♠
	4♥ 4♠	Dble	All pass

(1) A variation of Polish Club combined with a weak 1NT in which the 1♣ opening is either 18+ points, any shape, 15-17 balanced or 11-17 with clubs and not balanced.
(2) Negative free bid (6+ suit, not forcing)

Before choosing a lead, ask yourself, 'Which hand type will opener have for this sequence?' Clearly not the 18+ hand. With 15-17 balanced, opener would bid 4♥ with heart support, double for takeout otherwise. That means opener has a minimum opening with club length and probably only 3-card heart support.

It should be clear that your side has a double fit with nine hearts and at least nine clubs, a total of 18+ cards in hearts and clubs. It follows that the opponents must have 18+ cards in spades and diamonds.

The rule of suit length parity: *Whatever length you and partner have in your two longest combined suits, the opponents have the same total length in their two longest combined suits.*

This sounds pretty impressive but it is quite obvious. If in your 26 combined cards, you and partner have 18 cards in hearts-clubs, you have only 8 cards between you in spades-diamonds. Therefore the opponents must have 18 cards in spades-diamonds. This principle is important. If you have a double fit, so do the opponents.

Once you know the opponents have a double fit, you do not want to lead one of their suits (Tip 40). That simply helps declarer, whose plan will be 'draw trumps, set up second suit'. That means a trump lead is out and so is the $\Diamond$K. Partner cannot have length in clubs, support for hearts, enough spades to double them and also $\Diamond$A-x-x to give you a ruff.

Of your side's suits, the obvious choice is a heart. Lead the $\heartsuit$Q in case dummy has $\heartsuit$K-10. This was the full deal:

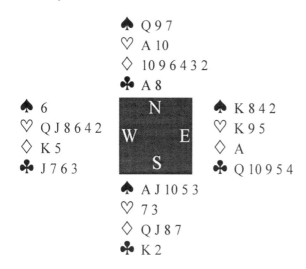

```
              ♠ Q 9 7
              ♡ A 10
              ◇ 10 9 6 4 3 2
              ♣ A 8
  ♠ 6            N          ♠ K 8 4 2
  ♡ Q J 8 6 4 2 W    E      ♡ K 9 5
  ◇ K 5                     ◇ A
  ♣ J 7 6 3      S          ♣ Q 10 9 5 4
              ♠ A J 10 5 3
              ♡ 7 3
              ◇ Q J 8 7
              ♣ K 2
```

As it happens, a heart lead is necessary to defeat the contract. If declarer draws all the trumps, via a finesse against East, declarer will lose control of the hand. If declarer draws two rounds of trumps and then starts on the diamonds, East wins, cashes the $\heartsuit$K and plays a third heart. Declarer can ruff this in hand and play another diamond. West wins and a fourth round of hearts will ensure a fourth defensive trick via the $\spadesuit$K, no matter where declarer ruffs.

At the table the $\Diamond$K lead was not a star-studded success and declarer wrapped up twelve tricks.

TIP 42:

In a trump contract do not lead from an ace-high suit, unless the suit is headed by the ace and king.

Leading from any suit headed by a single honour or broken honours is risky, leading from a suit headed by the ace without the king as well is the most dangerous. To lead such a suit is fine in no-trumps but in a suit contract it often results in giving a trick away.

(1)	8 7 4		(2)	10 9 6 3	
A 9 2		J 10 6 5	A 5 4		K Q
	K Q 3			J 8 7 2	

(3)	7 6 2		(4)	K 7 4	
A 5 4		Q 10 9 8	A 9 2		J 10 8 5
	K J 3			Q 6 3	

In each case if West leads the ace, South makes two tricks. If West does not lead the suit, South can be held to one trick.

In most cases declarer and dummy have the majority of points and an ace lead is more likely to set up tricks for declarer than for your side. Even ace-doubleton, seeking a ruff, is not likely to work. The original chance that partner has the king is one-in-three and if the opponents have far greater strength than partner, the odds are even worse.

Leading from an A-K suit has not yet set up any winners for declarer. After seeing dummy and partner's signal you can judge whether to continue the suit. If you must lead from an ace-high suit, start with the ace, not a low one, lest one opponent has a singleton king or the king is in one hand and there is a singleton in the other.

It may be reasonable to lead the ace from an ace-high suit:
- Against a pre-emptor, who is unlikely to have a vital outside king.
- When the bidding suggests partner will be able to ruff next round.
- Against a slam when you have a certain or very likely second trick.

Even so, if you never lead from an ace-high suit in a trump contract for the rest of your life, you will enjoy more success than regret.

TIP 43:

When dummy has revealed a long suit, lead an unbid suit. Unless you are very strong in dummy's suit, try to make an attacking lead. Do not lead trumps and do not lead dummy's long suit.

WEST
♠ 6 2
♡ A 8 7 3 2
◇ K 9 7 4
♣ 7 2

What should West lead after this auction?

WEST	NORTH	EAST	SOUTH
No	1♣	No	1♠
No	3♣	No	3♠
No	4♠	All pass	

When dummy has a long suit, declarer's normal plan is to draw trumps and use the long suit to discard losers. Leading trumps or the long suit aids declarer's plan. You must strive to score tricks in the unbid suits before declarer's losers can be discarded on dummy's suit.

Here the choice is hearts or diamonds. As you should not lead from an ace-high suit (Tip 42), start with the ◇4. The complete deal:

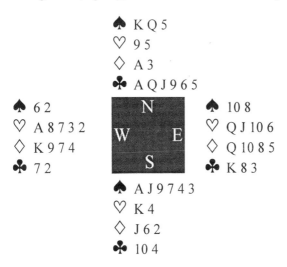

♠ K Q 5
♡ 9 5
◇ A 3
♣ A Q J 9 6 5

♠ 6 2
♡ A 8 7 3 2
◇ K 9 7 4
♣ 7 2

♠ 10 8
♡ Q J 10 6
◇ Q 10 8 5
♣ K 8 3

♠ A J 9 7 4 3
♡ K 4
◇ J 6 2
♣ 10 4

On the diamond lead, East will gain the lead at some time to push the ♡Q through to give the defence four tricks. A heart lead gives South the ♡K and declarer can also succeed on either black suit lead.

TIP 44:

Against a trump contract do not lead a singleton from a very strong hand.

WEST
♠ K 9 8 4
♡ A 7 3
♢ 6
♣ A Q 9 6 3

What should West lead after this auction?

WEST	NORTH	EAST	SOUTH
	1♢	No	1♡
Dble	2♢	No	3♡
No	4♡	All pass	

A singleton or a doubleton lead against a trump contract is best reserved for very weak hands. For a short suit lead to be useful, partner needs an entry to give you the ruff. With the strong opposition bidding and your own strong hand, partner can hardly have a quick entry. On a diamond lead, chances are that declarer will win, knock out your ♡A, draw trumps and discard black suit losers on dummy's diamonds. This is precisely what would happen on the actual deal:

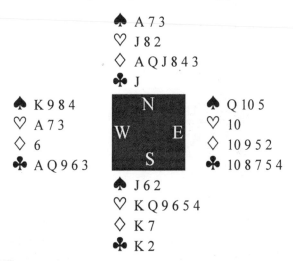

```
              ♠ A 7 3
              ♡ J 8 2
              ♢ A Q J 8 4 3
              ♣ J
♠ K 9 8 4          N          ♠ Q 10 5
♡ A 7 3                        ♡ 10
♢ 6          W         E      ♢ 10 9 5 2
♣ A Q 9 6 3       S           ♣ 10 8 7 5 4
              ♠ J 6 2
              ♡ K Q 9 6 5 4
              ♢ K 7
              ♣ K 2
```

A trump lead would be no better and is unwise when dummy has shown a long suit (Tip 43). A low spade is the best shot. If partner has the queen, it may be an entry to return a club (if, say, North held ♠A-x and ♣J-x) or a spade, whichever seems better.

TIP 45:

If dummy has not shown a long suit, then if you have no obviously attractive lead, prefer a passive lead to leading from a suit with just one honour or with two non-touching honours.

Sequences, suits headed by A-K or singletons are attractive leads. Attacking leads from suits like K-x-x-x, Q-x-x-x, J-x-x-x, K-J-x-x or similar are risky. A passive lead from three or more worthless cards or a trump lead from two or three rags is reasonably safe.

Suppose North opens 1NT and South jumps to 4♡. West to lead from:

    ♠ J 7 4   ♡ 8 6   ◇ A 9 7 5   ♣ 8 6 4 3

As dummy has not shown a long suit, an attacking lead is not needed. A diamond lead would be awful (Tip 42) and a spade lead is risky. A trump lead is reasonable but the best 'safe' lead is a club.

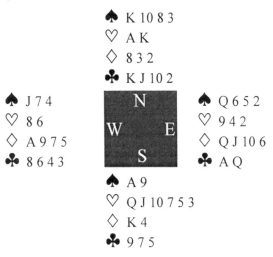

```
                    ♠ K 10 8 3
                    ♡ A K
                    ◇ 8 3 2
                    ♣ K J 10 2
  ♠ J 7 4              N              ♠ Q 6 5 2
  ♡ 8 6                               ♡ 9 4 2
  ◇ A 9 7 5         W     E           ◇ Q J 10 6
  ♣ 8 6 4 3            S              ♣ A Q
                    ♠ A 9
                    ♡ Q J 10 7 5 3
                    ◇ K 4
                    ♣ 9 7 5
```

The ◇A lead gives away a trick and a low spade can cost two tricks if declarer plays low from dummy and East plays the queen. A trump lead should result in one down but a club lead might do better: East wins the first two tricks and switches to the ◇Q. If South covers, West wins and the ◇9 next would be a thoughtful card. When it holds the trick, West should revert to clubs. East ruffs for two down.

TIP 46:

Trump length, lead length

When you hold four or more trumps and declarer has only five or six trumps, the best strategy can often be to force declarer to ruff and ruff again. If you can reduce declarer's trumps so that you hold more, you may be able to draw declarer's trumps or control the play by ruffing declarer's winners and playing your winners.

How can you force declarer to ruff? The best chance will usually be your long suit, since that is where declarer is likely to be shortish.

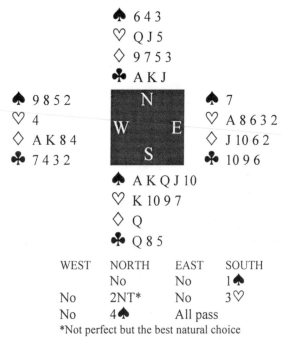

WEST	NORTH	EAST	SOUTH
	No	No	1♠
No	2NT*	No	3♡
No	4♠	All pass	

*Not perfect but the best natural choice

If West leads the ♡4, there is good news and bad news. East has the ♡A and West receives a ruff, but that is the end of the defence. If West starts with ◇A and continues diamonds, South ruffs and starts on trumps. Declarer receives the bad news on the second round of trumps but has no winning continuation.

If South draws West's trumps, there are two more diamond losers after conceding the ♡A. If South switches to hearts, East wins and should continue diamonds (if interested in a heart ruff, West would have led a heart). Once South ruffs, West has one trump more than South, who cannot escape two more losers. If South leads hearts, West ruffs and forces declarer again with the fourth diamond.

Here is a dramatic example of the 'forcing defence':

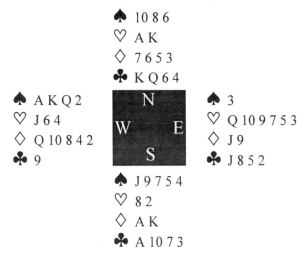

```
              ♠ 10 8 6
              ♡ A K
              ◇ 7 6 5 3
              ♣ K Q 6 4
♠ A K Q 2                      ♠ 3
♡ J 6 4          N            ♡ Q 10 9 7 5 3
◇ Q 10 8 4 2   W   E          ◇ J 9
♣ 9              S            ♣ J 8 5 2
              ♠ J 9 7 5 4
              ♡ 8 2
              ◇ A K
              ♣ A 10 7 3
```

South is in 4♠ after 1♠ : 2♣, 3♣ : 4♠. West is entitled to double as long as the best defence is produced. West should not lead the ♣9 (Tip 44). South wins and leads trumps at every opportunity until all the trumps are drawn. West scores just the ♠A-K-Q. Starting with a trump lead achieves the same result more quickly. On the basis of 'trump length, lead length' West should start with a diamond. If the club lead is a winner, West can always switch to a club later.

A diamond lead will beat 4♠ even though South has the diamonds well held. After diamond, won by South, trump won by West (if West ducks, that is that), diamond to South, trump to West, diamond ruffed, South has ♠J-9 while West has ♠A-2. If South leads another trump, that is two down: West wins and continues diamonds. The best South can do is to start on clubs and allow West to ruff for one down.

TIP 47:

If the bidding indicates that partner probably has four or more trumps, try to adopt a forcing defence to make declarer ruff.

Just as it pays to reduce declarer's trumps when you have trump length, likewise it is a sound approach when partner is marked with length in trumps.

WEST   What should West lead after this auction?

♠ 8 6 5
♡ 7
♢ K 8 7 6 2
♣ 10 7 3 2

WEST	NORTH	EAST	SOUTH
	No	No	1NT (15-17)
No	2♣	No	2♡
No	4♡	All pass	

It is likely that North-South are in a 4-4 heart fit. If so, East has four trumps and the recommended start is your long suit, a low diamond. Even then the defence will need to be very tight to defeat the contract.

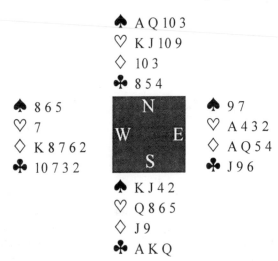

      ♠ A Q 10 3
      ♡ K J 10 9
      ♢ 10 3
      ♣ 8 5 4

♠ 8 6 5   ♠ 9 7
♡ 7   ♡ A 4 3 2
♢ K 8 7 6 2   ♢ A Q 5 4
♣ 10 7 3 2   ♣ J 9 6

      ♠ K J 4 2
      ♡ Q 8 6 5
      ♢ J 9
      ♣ A K Q

On any lead but a diamond, declarer wins and leads trumps. East's trumps can then be easily drawn and declarer has seven tricks in the black suits and three trump winners. If East holds off with the ♡A for three rounds, South abandons trumps and plays black suit winners.

On the low diamond lead East should play the $\diamondsuit$Q, although it is normally wrong to finesse against partner. South cannot hold a singleton $\diamondsuit$K and cannot quickly dispose of the diamond loser if holding $\diamondsuit$K-x. East can see from the points revealed that West has at most four points (see Tip 92). If the $\diamondsuit$Q loses, East can try a club when in with the $\heartsuit$A. When the $\diamondsuit$Q wins, it would be futile to switch to clubs as West, marked now with the $\diamondsuit$K, cannot hold a high honour in clubs.

East can see three tricks via two diamonds and a heart and with no additional high card tricks possible for East-West, the only remaining hope is an assault on the trump suit. After $\diamondsuit$Q, East cashes the $\diamondsuit$A and must play a third diamond, even though this concedes a ruff-and-discard. A ruff-and-sluff cannot hurt the defence if declarer's discards are winners anyway.

Declarer may ruff in either hand and start on trumps. It is now vital that East holds off with the $\heartsuit$A for two rounds. If the $\heartsuit$A is taken earlier, another diamond will be ruffed in the short hand and declarer can cross to the other hand and draw the remaining trumps.

Having held off for two rounds, East must win the third round of trumps. Now declarer and East each have one trump left. The fourth diamond either wins or forces declarer's last trump out. If declarer abandons trumps after two rounds, East will sooner or later ruff the third spade for one down.

If North-South reach 4$\spadesuit$ the demise would be much swifter. With a favourable trump break evident, West would lead the singleton heart. The play then goes $\heartsuit$A, heart ruff, diamond to the ace, heart ruff. That is already one down. If West cashes the $\diamondsuit$K, that is two down, while if West has the nerve to lead a low diamond to East's $\diamondsuit$Q, the contract goes three down. East would need to give suit-preference signals with the $\heartsuit$4 and $\heartsuit$3 and West would need to be alert enough to read this as asking for the higher non-trump suit, diamonds.

TIP 48:

Except in special circumstances, do not lead a singleton trump.

Trumps leads are not normally recommended if dummy has not shown support for declarer's suit. If dummy may be void or have a singleton in declarer's suit, leading a trump may simply trap partner's trick. For example, if the opponents have bid 1♠ : 1NT, 3♠ : Pass, a spade lead from two or three low trumps would cost in these layouts:

```
          4                           - - -
  7 2             J 8 6 5      7 5 4           Q 10 6 2
        A K Q 10 9 3                  A K J 9 8 3
```

When dummy has shown support and no long suit, a trump lead may be attractive but if you have one trump, partner often has three or four. You may well destroy partner's trick if you lead your trump.

```
        K 6 4 2          Declarer's normal play is king then
  7              Q 10 5  ace and partner's queen would score
        A J 9 8 3        a trick, but not if you lead the suit.
```

```
        K 6 4            With no intimation of a bad break,
  7              J 10 5 2 declarer would start with two top
        A Q 9 8 3        trumps and East scores a trick.
```

If West leads a trump, low, ten, ace, South plays back to the king. With the bad break revealed, South finesses against East.

When might you lead a singleton trump?

• If partner passes a takeout double at the 1-level, thereby revealing better trumps than declarer, a trump lead, even if singleton, is expected.

• When partner makes a penalty double of a suit at the 1-level.

• When your side is strong in all three suits outside trumps.

• Against a sacrifice bid or when your side has clearly more high card strength than their side.

TIP 49:

Lead trumps against sacrifice bids, even a singleton trump.

WEST
♠ A 7
♡ A K J 5 2
♢ 9 4 3
♣ A 7 6

What should West lead after this auction?

WEST	NORTH	EAST	SOUTH
1♡	2NT*	4♡	5♣
Dble	No	No	No

*Both minors, at least 5-5

When your side clearly has the greater strength, how will declarer take tricks at a level higher than justified by the high card values? Only by ruffing. The best defence to maximise the penalty is to lead trumps at every opportunity.

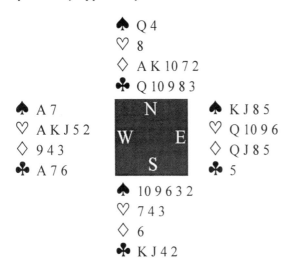

```
              ♠ Q 4
              ♡ 8
              ♢ A K 10 7 2
              ♣ Q 10 9 8 3
♠ A 7                        ♠ K J 8 5
♡ A K J 5 2      N           ♡ Q 10 9 6
♢ 9 4 3      W     E         ♢ Q J 8 5
♣ A 7 6          S           ♣ 5
              ♠ 10 9 6 3 2
              ♡ 7 4 3
              ♢ 6
              ♣ K J 4 2
```

West leads a low club (in case East has a ♣K singleton). Declarer wins and plays ♢A, ♢K, diamond ruff. Now West cannot be prevented from gaining the lead and ♣A and another club removes South's trumps. East will score a diamond trick to take 5♣ three down.

It is tempting to lead a top heart to take a look at dummy but in an auction like this, it can be a costly look. After a heart lead, declarer can escape for two down even if West shifts to ♣A and another club.

TIP 50:

Lead trumps if declarer has shown a two-suiter and you are strong in declarer's second suit.

WEST	What should West lead after this auction?
♠ A Q 10 7	
♡ 5 4 3	
◇ K 9	
♣ J 10 9 2	

WEST	NORTH	EAST	SOUTH
		No	1♠
No	1NT	No	2♡
No	No	No	

Rather than start with the 'automatic' ♣J, reflect on the bidding. As North passed 2♡, there will be more hearts in dummy than spades. Declarer will be planning to ruff spades in dummy. To minimise such ruffs you should lead trumps as early and as often as possible.

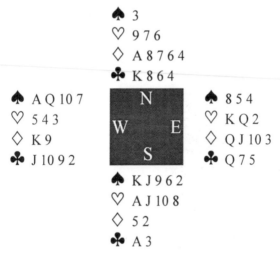

```
                      ♠ 3
                      ♡ 9 7 6
                      ◇ A 8 7 6 4
                      ♣ K 8 6 4

♠ A Q 10 7            N              ♠ 8 5 4
♡ 5 4 3         W          E         ♡ K Q 2
◇ K 9                                ◇ Q J 10 3
♣ J 10 9 2            S              ♣ Q 7 5

                      ♠ K J 9 6 2
                      ♡ A J 10 8
                      ◇ 5 2
                      ♣ A 3
```

On a club lead, declarer would win in dummy and lead the ♠3. West would win but the trump switch would be too late. South wins, ruffs a spade, comes to the ♣A and ruffs another spade. Declarer scores two spade ruffs, three hearts in hand and three minor suit winners.

On a trump lead, the defence can play three rounds of trumps before declarer can ruff a spade. Declarer then has only three trump tricks and three minor suit winners.

TIP 51:

Lead trumps when one opponent has shown a freak two-suiter and the other has given a preference.

WEST

♠ A K J 2
♡ Q 10
◇ A K J 10 6 5
♣ 2

What should West lead after this auction?

WEST	NORTH	EAST	SOUTH
1◇	2NT*	No	3♣
3♠	5♣	All pass	

*Hearts and clubs, at least 5-5

You are permitted to double 5♣ as long as you find the right defence. Clearly North has a powerful two-suiter, as North went on to game despite no enthusiasm by South. As South preferred clubs you can assume South will have more clubs than hearts. To preserve any heart tricks that belong to your side, lead a trump, even though it is a singleton.

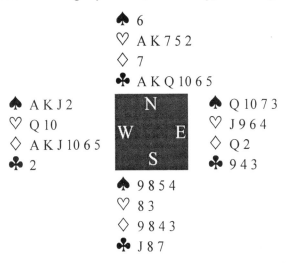

♠ 6
♡ A K 7 5 2
◇ 7
♣ A K Q 10 6 5

♠ A K J 2	**N**	♠ Q 10 7 3
♡ Q 10	**W E**	♡ J 9 6 4
◇ A K J 10 6 5		◇ Q 2
♣ 2	**S**	♣ 9 4 3

♠ 9 8 5 4
♡ 8 3
◇ 9 8 4 3
♣ J 8 7

In practice West led a top spade but that was fatal. The trump switch was too late. South won and played ♡A, ♡K, heart ruff, spade ruff, heart ruff. Declarer lost just one spade and one diamond.

On a trump lead, declarer can play ♡A, ♡K, heart ruff, but now there is no convenient entry to dummy. East can win either red suit exit and lead a trump. The defence will now score a heart trick as well.

TIP 52:

**Lead trumps when your side is known to be strong in the three
suits outside trumps.**

WEST
♠ K Q 6 4
♡ Q 9
◇ A Q 9 8 2
♣ 6 4

What should West lead after this auction?

WEST	NORTH	EAST	SOUTH
1◇	No	1♡	2♣
No	No	No	

It is tempting to lead partner's suit but a 1-level response has no lead-
directing element. No suit quality is required for a response. As you are
so strong in spades and diamonds, it is unlikely that any heart tricks will
be lost if you start with a trump lead.

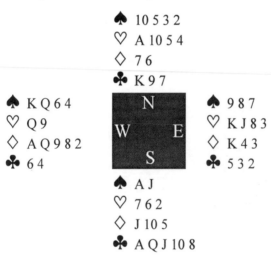

♠ 10 5 3 2
♡ A 10 5 4
◇ 7 6
♣ K 9 7

♠ K Q 6 4
♡ Q 9
◇ A Q 9 8 2
♣ 6 4

♠ 9 8 7
♡ K J 8 3
◇ K 4 3
♣ 5 3 2

♠ A J
♡ 7 6 2
◇ J 10 5
♣ A Q J 10 8

East-West would do quite well in diamonds but the matter at hand is
the defence to 2♣. If West leads a trump, South can be held to five
trumps and two aces, one off. If South tries for a diamond ruff, West
wins and leads another trump. West allows East to win the next
diamond to lead a third trump. If declarer wins the second trump in
dummy to lead a diamond, East must rise with the ◇K. If West wins
the second diamond, West does not have a third trump.

If West had started with the ♡Q lead, South could take the ♡A and play a diamond. The defence could no longer prevent the diamond ruff, which gives declarer eight tricks. The ♠K lead is also fatal.

WEST
♠ 8 7 5
♡ K J 10 9
◇ 7 2
♣ A Q 9 7

What should West lead after this auction?

WEST	NORTH	EAST	SOUTH
		3◇	3♠
No	4♠	All pass	

West's trumps are too weak and diamonds too long to hope for a stunning success with a diamond lead. As West is so strong in clubs and hearts, while East figures to have good diamonds, a trump lead is likely to be best.

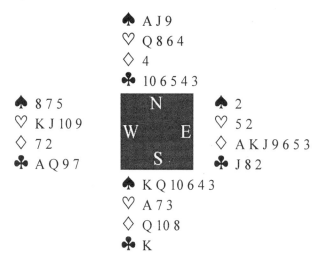

♠ A J 9
♡ Q 8 6 4
◇ 4
♣ 10 6 5 4 3

♠ 8 7 5
♡ K J 10 9
◇ 7 2
♣ A Q 9 7

♠ 2
♡ 5 2
◇ A K J 9 6 5 3
♣ J 8 2

♠ K Q 10 6 4 3
♡ A 7 3
◇ Q 10 8
♣ K

On a diamond lead, East wins but the trump switch is too late. South wins, ruffs a diamond, crosses to the ♡A and ruffs a diamond. A club exit would see South losing only one heart, one club and one diamond.

If West leads a trump won in dummy, East wins the diamond and whether East shifts to clubs or hearts, West will be able to lead a second trump. Declarer can then ruff only one diamond in dummy and careful defence should give East-West one heart, two diamonds and a club.

TIP 53:

If the opponents have reached a 4-3 or 4-4 trump fit and you hold five rag trumps, lead a trump.

WEST
♠ A K J 10 9
♡ A
♢ 9 5 4 3 2
♣ Q 2

What should West lead after this auction?

WEST	NORTH	EAST	SOUTH
1♠	Dble	No	3♢
No	No	No	

A 4-3 trump fit plays reasonably if declarer is able to ruff in the short trump hand. The strength of the 4-4 fit is declarer's ability to ruff in either hand and retain trump length in the other. In both cases, you can minimise declarer's ruffing capacity by repeated trump leads.

When declarer has 5-6 trumps, a forcing defence can be best (Tip 46). If declarer has fewer than five trumps and you have five, lead a trump.

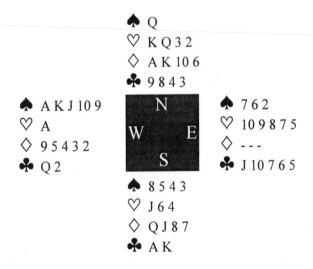

```
            ♠ Q
            ♡ K Q 3 2
            ♢ A K 10 6
            ♣ 9 8 4 3
♠ A K J 10 9                    ♠ 7 6 2
♡ A              N              ♡ 10 9 8 7 5
♢ 9 5 4 3 2   W     E           ♢ - - -
♣ Q 2            S              ♣ J 10 7 6 5
            ♠ 8 5 4 3
            ♡ J 6 4
            ♢ Q J 8 7
            ♣ A K
```

If West leads a trump, declarer can be beaten. West can lead another trump when in with a spade or the ♡A and hold declarer to eight tricks. In practice West led a spade and switched to a trump but that was too late. Declarer could ruff three spades in dummy and make 3♢.

TIP 54:

A trump lead is often best when the opponents are playing in their third-bid trump suit or their fourth-bid suit.

WEST		What should West lead after this auction?	
♠ 6 4			
♡ Q 9 8 7 3	WEST	NORTH	EAST	SOUTH
◇ K Q			No	1◇
♣ 10 9 8 5	No	1♡	No	1♠
	No	4♠	All pass	

When the opponents bid two suits and end in the third-bid suit, it often indicates a cross-ruff is likely. Each opponent may be short in the first suit bid by partner. The best defence to a cross-ruff is a trump lead and more trumps at every opportunity. On this reasoning West should lead a trump.

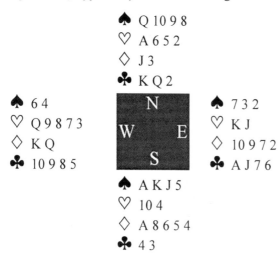

```
              ♠ Q 10 9 8
              ♡ A 6 5 2
              ◇ J 3
              ♣ K Q 2
 ♠ 6 4           N          ♠ 7 3 2
 ♡ Q 9 8 7 3   W   E        ♡ K J
 ◇ K Q           S          ◇ 10 9 7 2
 ♣ 10 9 8 5                 ♣ A J 7 6
              ♠ A K J 5
              ♡ 10 4
              ◇ A 8 6 5 4
              ♣ 4 3
```

On a trump lead, South may win and duck a diamond. A second trump follows and declarer continues with ◇A and a diamond ruff. Now declarer cannot leave dummy without allowing East to gain the lead and play a deadly third round of trumps. This leaves declarer one trick short. It is true that a club lead to the king and ace followed by a trump switch also works but do not expect partner to do the right thing when you could have done it first yourself.

TIP 55:

Listen to the bidding. If the opponents bid and raise a suit, they usually have at least eight cards between them.

What should West lead after each of these auctions?

(A) WEST	WEST	NORTH	EAST	SOUTH
♠ A 6			No	1♡
♡ 7 5 4	No	2◇	No	3◇
◇ A 9 3 2	No	3♡	No	4♡
♣ J 9 3 2	No	No	No	

(B) WEST	WEST	NORTH	EAST	SOUTH
♠ Q 5			No	1♡
♡ 8 7 2	No	2◇	No	3◇
◇ 9 8 6 5 2	No	4♡	All pass	
♣ A 7 6				

(C) WEST	WEST	NORTH	EAST	SOUTH
♠ A 6			No	1♠
♡ 8 5 2	No	3♣	No	4♣
◇ J 10 9 3	No	4♠	No	4NT
♣ 7 4 3 2	No	5♡	No	6♠ End

(D) WEST	WEST	NORTH	EAST	SOUTH
♠ J 10 2			No	1◇
♡ A 6	No	2NT	No	3♡
◇ J 8 7 4 3	No	4♡	All pass	
♣ K 8 2				

(E) WEST	WEST	NORTH	EAST	SOUTH
♠ K 6				1♠
♡ 10 9 8 6	No	2♣	No	2♡
◇ Q 8 5 2	No	2NT*	No	3♡
♣ Q 9 3	No	4♠	No	4NT
	No	5♠	No	6♠ End

*Forcing to game

84

(A) North-South appear to hold eight diamonds, leaving partner with a singleton. Lead the $\diamond$A and continue with the *nine* of diamonds for partner to ruff. The $\diamond$9 asks for a spade return (high card for the high suit when giving a ruff). You expect to take $\diamond$A, diamond ruff, ♠A, diamond ruff plus any further tricks partner can contribute.

(B) If the opposition bidding is natural, North-South have shown eight diamonds and so partner figures to be void. Lead the *two* of diamonds, asking partner to return a club (lowest card, lowest suit excluding trumps). The normal rule for leads (fourth-highest, M.U.D., etc.) do not apply when you expect partner to ruff the lead. You plan to take a diamond ruff, ♣A and another diamond ruff and hope partner has at least one more trick.

(C) The opposition bidding suggests they have eight clubs, leaving partner with at most a singleton. Lead a club and, on gaining the lead with the ♠A give partner a club ruff.

(D) South's bidding suggests 5 diamonds – 4 hearts. North's 2NT promises at least 2 diamonds, leaving partner with at most a singleton. Dig a little deeper and it is likely partner has no diamonds. North presumably has four hearts but why did North bid 2NT and not 1$\heartsuit$? Probably because the hand pattern is 3-4-3-3. If that is so and South has five diamonds, East is void. Lead the $\diamond$3, asking for a club return (low card, low suit).

(E) South has shown at least 5-5 in the majors. With 2-2 in the majors North would rebid 3NT over 3$\heartsuit$. With 2 spades – 3 hearts, North would raise to 4$\heartsuit$. The jump to 4♠ should have 3 spades, but why did North choose 2NT over 2$\heartsuit$ instead of 4♠ or a forcing 3♠? You might reasonably deduce that North is 3-3-3-4. That leaves East with a singleton heart and you should lead a heart.

The deal arose in the 2002 IOC Teams prior to the Olympic Winter Games in Salt Lake City. A heart lead would have defeated the slam. East had a singleton and three trumps and West could give East a heart ruff when in with the ♠K. The slam made on a diamond lead.

TIPS 56-80: Declarer play

TIP 56:

Apply the Even Suit Break Test when deciding whether to play for the drop or to finesse.

Some hands require no more than a key suit be handled to best advantage. You need to know the correct technique for handling basic card combinations. Once the correct technique is second nature, you can progress to judging when to depart from the 'book' play.

The Even Suit Break Test

Step 1: Assume the missing cards divide as even as possible.

Step 2: Assume the missing honour is with the longer holding if there is an odd number of cards missing. If the even-break is 3-2, place the missing key card with the 3-card holding; if the even-break is 2-1, assume the missing card is doubleton, not singleton.

Step 3: Check whether the missing honour will drop if you play your suit from the top and the even-break occurs. If the honour placed with the longer holding will not drop, take the finesse.

Of course, the play based on this approach will not work all the time but it gives you the best chance for success if you do not have any inkling as to which opponent holds the missing honour.

Should you finesse or play for the drop with these combinations:

Dummy	(1) 8 6 5 4	(2) 8 6 5 4 3	(3) 8 6 5 4 3
Declarer	A Q 9 7 2	A Q 9 7 2	A Q J 9 7 2

Solutions: (1) 4 cards missing – even-break 2-2 – king figures to be doubleton – king unlikely to fall under the ace – take the finesse.

(2) 3 cards missing – even-break 2-1 – king figures to be doubleton – king unlikely to fall under the ace – take the finesse.

(3) 2 cards missing – even-break 1-1 – king likely to be singleton – probably will fall under the ace – play the ace rather than finesse.

What is the best play with these combinations?

Dummy	(4) A 6 4 2	(5) A 6 4 2	(6) 9 8 6 4 2
Declarer	K J 7 3	K J 7 5 3	A K J 5 3

Solutions: (4) 5 cards missing – even-break 3-2 – queen will be with the tripleton more often than the doubleton – queen is thus unlikely to fall if you play ace and king – best is to finesse: ace first, then low to the jack. When finessing for a queen, it is usual to finesse on the second round of the suit (ace or king first, finesse on the next round).

(5) 4 cards missing – even-break 2-2 – queen likely to be doubleton – queen is thus likely to fall if you play ace and king – reject the finesse.

(6) 3 cards missing – even-break 2-1 – queen likely to be doubleton – do not finesse on the first round (could lose to queen singleton). Play the ace: if all follow, the queen will fall under the king; if LHO shows out, cross to dummy in another suit and finesse the jack; if RHO shows out, you have a loser . . . somebody up there does not like you.

How do you manage these holdings to give yourself the best chance of avoiding a loser?

Dummy	(7) 8 4	(8) 8 4	(9) 4
Declarer	A K Q 10 6 2	A K Q 10 6	A K Q 10 2

Solutions: (7) 5 cards missing – even-break 3-2 – jack likely to be tripleton – play ace, king, queen – do not finesse the ten.

(8) 6 cards missing – even-break 3-3 – jack likely to be tripleton – play ace, king, queen – do not finesse the ten.

(9) 7 cards missing – even-break is 4-3 – J-x-x-x is more likely than J-x-x. The jack is therefore not likely to drop if you play ace, king, queen. The best chance for maximum tricks is to finesse the ten.

Caution: The correct technique for one particular suit may not be the correct approach to the whole hand. Other considerations may apply.

TIP 57:

When cashing winners in a suit, keep the tenace and the near-tenace intact. First play the winners opposite the tenace.

Tenace: Non-touching honours in the same suit (A-Q, A-J, A-10, K-J, K-10, Q-10), where the opponents hold the card(s) in-between your honours. More broadly, any two cards near in rank (such as J-9, Q-9, 10-8, 9-7) where the in-between card(s) are held by the opposition.

A tenace gives you the opportunity to take a finesse. If you have a tenace in a suit where you have winners in dummy and winners in hand, play first the winners where there is no tenace. Retain the tenace as long as you can. This helps to guard against bad breaks.

What is the best play with these holdings?

Dummy	(1) A J 6 4 2	(2) A 9 6 4 2	(3) A J 9 2
Declarer	K 8 7 5 3	K J 7 5 3	K 7 5 4 3

Solutions: (1) Play the king first – retain the A-J tenace – guards against Q-10-9 with LHO. If RHO has Q-10-9, a loser is inevitable.

(2) Play the ace first – retain the K-J tenace – guards against Q-10-9 with RHO. If LHO has Q-10-9, a loser is inevitable.

(3) Play the king first – retain the A-J-9 double tenace. If all follow, play the ace next (Tip 56), but if RHO shows out, you can finesse the nine next and the jack later to lose no tricks despite the 4-0 break.

How about these combinations?

Dummy	(4) A 10 6 2	(5) A Q 4 2	(6) Q 10 5 4
Declarer	K Q 5 3	K 10 5 3	A K 7 3

Solutions: (4) Play the K-Q first – retain the A-10 tenace – guards against J-x-x-x with LHO. If RHO has J-x-x-x, a loser is inevitable.

(5) Play the A-Q first – retain the K-10 tenace.

(6) Play the A-K first – retain the Q-10 tenace.

If there is no obvious tenace, there is still a correct order in which winners should be cashed. Check the winners in your hand and dummy and note which hand contains the card closest to a winner. Treat that combination as a 'near-tenace' and play first the winners from the other hand. Keep the near-tenace intact as long as possible.

Dummy	K Q 3 2	In which order should you play
Declarer	A 9 5 4	your winners?

The nearest card to winning rank is the 9 – treat A-9 as a near- tenace. Play first the king and queen. If the suit breaks 3-2, your foresight was unnecessary. Your reward comes when the layout is like this:

	K Q 3 2		If you play the ace on the first or
J		10 8 7 6	second round (breaking your tenace),
	A 9 5 4		RHO wins a trick with the 10.

By playing K-Q, West shows out on the second round and with A-9 over the 10-8, you can finesse the 9 for no loser.

Dummy	A 7 3 2	How you handle this suit to lose
Declarer	K 9 5 4	only one trick if possible?

The 9 is closer to winning rank than the 7. Therefore retain the K-9 initially and play the ace first. If only low cards fall, play the king next and hope the suit breaks 3-2. If LHO drops an honour, lead low next and insert the 9 if East plays low.

	A 7 3 2		If the suit breaks 3-2, the 9 loses but
Q J		10 8 6	the king captures the missing card on
	K 9 5 4		the next round.

Your reward comes on a division like this:

	A 7 3 2		If you play the king first (breaking
J		Q 10 8 5	the near-tenace) RHO has two tricks.
	K 9 5 4		Start with the ace.

When the jack drops, play low towards your K-9. If East plays the 8, your 9 wins and you lose only one trick. If East plays an honour, you take it. When West shows out, cross to dummy in another suit to lead towards your 9-6, restricting RHO's Q-8 to one trick.

TIP 58:

When missing J-10-x-x or J-x-x-x, if you hold equivalent tenaces or near-tenaces, retain as many winners in one hand as there are missing honours.

These situations are treated identically:

Dummy	(1) K 10 4 3	(2) K Q 10 3	(3) Q 9 4 3
Declarer	A Q 9 5 2	A 9 5 4 2	A K 10 6 2

In each case you have three winners and, as the 10 and 9 are equivalent, the K-10 tenace is equivalent to the A-9 or Q-9 tenace. As you are missing only *one* honour, keep *one* winner in each hand. Therefore, in (1), play the ace or queen first, not the king; in (2), play the king or queen first, not the ace; and in (3), play the ace or king first, not the queen. This guards against a 4-0 break against either opponent.

These situations are treated identically:

Dummy	(4) K Q 9 2	(5) A Q 8 3 2	(6) Q 8 3 2
Declarer	A 8 5 4 3	K 9 5 4	A K 9 5 4

In each case you have three winners. The 9 and 8 produce equivalent near-tenaces. This time, as *two* honours are missing, you must retain *two* honours to capture the jack and ten if the suit does break 4-0. Thus in (4), play the ace first. If LHO does have J-10-7-6, you can lead twice towards the K-Q-9 to avoid a loser. In (5), play the king first, retaining the A-Q-8 in case LHO has J-10-7-6. In (6), play the queen first to cater for J-10-7-6 with RHO.

```
            Q 8 3 2          If a 4-0 break exists but the J-10-x-x
  J 10 7 6            - - -  lie over your two honours, you are
            A K 9 5 4        unable to escape a loser.
```

If you lead low from hand, West can simply play the jack or ten to ensure a trick.

TIP 59:

When more than one suit offers the chance to make your contract and it is dangerous to lose the lead, first try those possibilities which do not risk losing the lead.

(1) WEST	EAST		West is in 3NT with no
♠ 7 6 3	♠ K 4		opposition bidding. North
♡ A K 3	♡ Q 5 4 2		leads the ♠5 and dummy's
◇ A 4	◇ K Q 10 2		king wins. Phew. How would
♣ A Q 9 4 3	♣ J 10 5		you continue as West?

(2) WEST	EAST		West is in 6NT with no
♠ A K J 9	♠ 10 3		opposition bidding. North
♡ A 9 4	♡ J 5		leads the ♡K. How would
◇ A 6 2	◇ K Q 9 4 3		you plan the play?
♣ A J 3	♣ K Q 10 4		

Solutions: (1) After the ♠K holds, you have eight top winners. The 'instinctive' club finesse is too risky just yet. If it loses, you have no further chance to test either red suit for the ninth trick.

Try the hearts first. If they are 3-3, your ninth trick has materialised. If hearts are not 3-3, try the diamonds next, ace, king, queen. This is not a case for finessing the ◇10 (see Tip 56). If the ◇J has dropped, the ◇10 is high. If hearts are not 3-3 and the ◇J has not appeared, lead the ♣J and let it run if South plays low. The club finesse is *the last resort.*

(2) You have ten top tricks. The two extra can come from two spade finesses or a favourable diamond break. As you have no entry problems, you may as well run your club winners and discard a heart. Defenders do sometimes discard badly. Follow with a diamond to the ace and a diamond to the king, keeping your Q-9 near-tenace. If the diamonds are 3-2 or if South started with the ◇10 or ◇J bare, you have five diamond tricks.

If the diamonds do not behave, lead the ♠10 and let it run, repeating the finesse if it works. With two cards opposite A-K-J-10, A-K-J-10-x or A-K-J-10-x-x (or equivalent holdings), it is better to finesse for the queen on the first round of the suit.

TIP 60:

Declarer should normally win or attempt to win a trick with the highest of equal cards.

Dummy
642

West leads the 5.   East plays the jack.

A K Q
Declarer

In no-trumps, where declarer is likely to hold up with A-x or A-x-x, it may be better to win with the king. Otherwise, declarer should win with the ace. It is immaterial to declarer, as the A, K and Q are all winners. By winning with the ace you make it harder for the defenders to know who holds the missing honours. Suppose this is the actual layout:

642

10 8 7 5 3   J 9

A K Q

If you win with the queen, West deduces that you hold the ace and king as the jack is East's highest. West may later switch to a suit more dangerous to you. If you win with the ace, West must consider whether the position is as above or perhaps one of these two:

642   642

10 8 7 5 3   Q J   OR   10 8 7 5 3   K Q J

A K 9   A 9

In each case, East's correct play is the jack. Third hand plays high but should play the cheapest of equally high cards. If you make the defenders regularly guess at the layout, sometimes they will guess wrongly.

Similarly:

8 3

West leads the 4.   East plays the 10.

A Q J

Win with the queen, not with the jack.

7 5

West leads the 3.   East plays the 9.

A K J 10

Win with the jack, not with the ten.

The same principle applies when you are taking a finesse with equal cards in hand:

Dummy   7 4 3   You lead the 3 from dummy, East
                             plays the 2 and you play . . .?
Declarer   A Q J 10 5

The correct card is the queen. If the finesse works it is irrelevant to you whether you finesse the queen, jack or ten. If the finesse loses, the actual card chosen is also irrelevant to you, but in each case it is not irrelevant to the defenders. By finessing the queen you obscure the location of the jack and ten.

Suppose the position is:

7 4 3

9 6   K 8 2

A Q J 10 5

If you finesse the ten and it holds the trick, East knows that West cannot have the queen or the jack. If you finesse the queen and it holds, East cannot be sure who has the jack or the ten.

There are similar considerations if the position is:

7 4 3

K 9   8 6 2

A Q J 10 5

If you finesse the ten and West wins with the king, East can tell that West does not have the queen or jack. Since a defender wins with the cheapest card possible, winning with the king denies the queen and jack. If you finesse the queen and West wins with the king, East cannot tell who has the jack or ten.

The more you keep them guessing, the more mistakes they will make.

TIP 61:

When a ruff is threatened and you are certain or likely to lose the lead in trumps, it can benefit you to eliminate an irrelevant side suit before touching trumps. If the ruff eventuates, the player on lead may have no safe exit.

WEST	EAST
♠ A Q 7	♠ 8 3
♡ Q 8 6 2	♡ K 10 9 5 4 3
◇ A 7 3	◇ K 8
♣ K Q 3	♣ 9 8 7

West is in 4♡ (no opposition bidding). North leads the ♣6, South plays the ♣10 and you win with the ♣K. How would you continue?

This was the complete deal from the 1996 Australian Women's Teams:

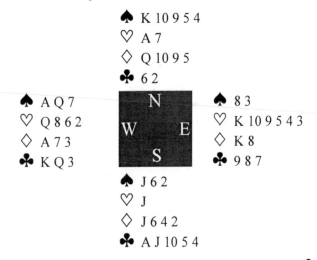

South did well to duck the first club. If South takes the ♣A, there is no defence. It is tempting to play a trump at trick 2. If you do, North wins, plays a second club to South's ace and scores a club ruff. After a diamond exit, you are one down when the spade finesse loses.

Spotting the danger of the club ruff (why else would South duck the first club), Tina Zines first played ◇K, ◇A , diamond ruff and then led a trump to the queen and ace. North played the ♣2 to South's ace and ruffed the club return but was then end-played.

As North had to lead a spade or give declarer a ruff-and-discard, West's spade loser was eliminated. Stripping the diamonds left North with no safe exit.

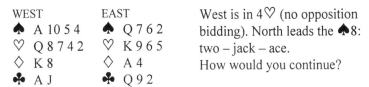

WEST   EAST

♠ A 10 5 4   ♠ Q 7 6 2

♡ Q 8 7 4 2   ♡ K 9 6 5

♢ K 8   ♢ A 4

♣ A J   ♣ Q 9 2

West is in 4♡ (no opposition bidding). North leads the ♠8: two – jack – ace. How would you continue?

The deal arose in the 2002 New Zealand Open Teams:

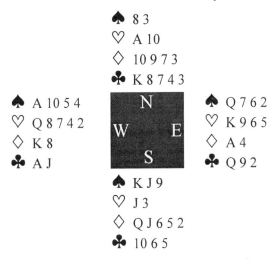

As the cards lie, it would work to duck the ♠J at trick 1 but that could be foolish. What if South returned a low spade? To rise with the ♠A could see it ruffed. If you play low, what if North has led from ♠K-9-8? North wins and South ruffs the next spade.

Those who played a trump at trick 2 paid the price. North took the ace, played a second spade and ruffed the spade return. North later scored a club trick and declarer was one down.

After taking the ♠A, declarer should cash the ♢A and ♢K and only then lead a trump. North can take the ♡A, play a spade and receive a spade ruff but is then end-played. A club or a diamond exit removes declarer's club loser.

TIP 62:

As soon as dummy appears, count dummy's high card points and your own. Deduct the total from 40 and you can often tell where the missing points are.

(1)

	WEST	EAST	WEST	NORTH	EAST	SOUTH
♠	K J 9 8 5	♠ A Q 4		1♡	1NT	No
♡	J 2	♡ A K	3♠	No	4♠	All pass
◇	6 5 4	◇ Q J 10				
♣	A Q 4	♣ 8 7 6 3 2				

North leads ◇A, ◇K and a third diamond. All follow. Plan the play.

(2)

	WEST	EAST	WEST	NORTH	EAST	SOUTH
♠	K 10 8 4	♠ Q J 7 2		1♡	Dble	No
♡	A 3	♡ J 2	2♠	No	4♠	All pass
◇	J 7 5 2	◇ A K Q				
♣	Q 7 4	♣ K 6 5 3				

North leads the ♡K, won by your ace. A spade is won by North who cashes the ♡Q and exits with a spade, South following. North discards a heart on the next spade. Plan the rest of the play.

(1) You have 11 HCP, dummy has 16 HCP. 40 − 27 = 13 HCP are missing. North should have almost all of these points for the opening bid. The ♣K will therefore be with North and finessing the ♣Q will lose. Do not take a finesse that is known to fail (see Tip 63). Draw trumps and continue with ♣A and a low club, hoping that North began with ♣K singleton or doubleton. If North began with something like ♠ 7 3 ♡ Q 10 9 5 4 3 ◇ A K 8 ♣ K 9, you will make your game, which would fail if you finessed the ♣Q.

(2) You have 10 HCP and dummy has 16 HCP. That leaves 14 HCP for the opponents. You have lost two tricks and must lose a club trick. You can afford to lose one club but not two. As North opened the bidding, you can place North with the ♣A, else North would have opened with only 10 HCP. Your only legitimate chance is that North has the ♣A singleton or doubleton.

Win the third spade in hand and lead a low club towards dummy's king. If North's ace appears, your problems are over. If North plays low and the ♣K wins, continue with a club from dummy and play low from your hand. Do not play the queen. If you play the ♣Q and it loses, their ♣J or ♣10 will be high. You have to hope that North started with something like ♠ A 3 ♡ K Q 10 9 6 4 ◇ 8 6 3 ♣ A 9. When you duck the second club, the ♣A falls and your ♣Q will be high. The key is not to lose either of your club honours to the ace.

If North began with ♣A-x-x or ♣A-x-x-x or longer, your contract never had a real chance. Your only legitimate hope is that North has the ♣A short.

WEST	EAST	Pairs : Both vulnerable			
♠ A K 8 6 5 2	♠ 9 7 3	WEST	NORTH	EAST	SOUTH
♡ 6 3 2	♡ 8 5 4			No	No
◇ J 6 2	◇ A 5 3	2♠	No	No	No
♣ 8	♣ A Q J 2				

North leads the ♡J against 2♠, a weak-two opening. South takes the ♡Q, ♡K, ♡A and switches to the ◇10. You win with the ◇A in dummy and cash the ♠A, ♠K.

How would you plan the play at match-pointed pairs if (a) trumps are 3-1, with South having the ♠Q singleton, or (b) if trumps are 2-2 with South having ♠Q-10? What precautions have you taken so far?

The precautions you should have taken are not to play the ◇J on the ◇10 and to play the ♠9 on the first or second round of spades to unblock the suit.

You began with 8 HCP, dummy with 11 HCP and South has shown up with 11 HCP in each case. The remaining 10 HCP must be with North, as South failed to open the bidding and has already turned up with 11 points.

(a) If trumps are 3-1, you should continue by finessing the ♣Q, which is sure to succeed. You discard a diamond loser on the ♣A and just make your contract. If North happened to start with ♣K-x, the ♣K drops and you can throw your remaining diamond on the ♣J.

WEST	EAST	Pairs : Both vulnerable

```
WEST          EAST          Pairs : Both vulnerable
♠ A K 8 6 5 2  ♠ 9 7 3       WEST NORTH EAST SOUTH
♡ 6 3 2        ♡ 8 5 4                  No    No
◇ J 6 2        ◇ A 5 3       2♠   No    No    No
♣ 8            ♣ A Q J 2
```

(b) North leads the ♡J and South takes the ♡Q, ♡K, ♡A and switches to the ◇10. You win with the ◇A in dummy and cash the ♠A, ♠K. Trumps are 2-2 and South turns up with ♠Q-10.

Here, too, you can safely take the club finesse and that will score an overtrick for you. Should you be satisfied with that?

As North is marked with ◇K-Q and the ♣K, you are able to squeeze North (and that is why you did not play your ◇J on the ◇10). Play two more spades and you will reach an ending like this:

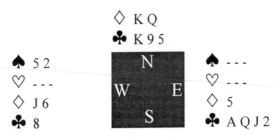

```
              ◇ K Q
              ♣ K 9 5
♠ 5 2                      ♠ - - -
♡ - - -                    ♡ - - -
◇ J 6                      ◇ 5
♣ 8                        ♣ A Q J 2
```

Immaterial

Play off the ♠5 and ♠2, discarding the ◇5 and ♣2 from dummy. If North lets go both diamond honours, take your ◇J and the club finesse for ten tricks. If North lets go one diamond and one club, finesse the club, cash the ♣A, dropping the king, and cash dummy's last club for ten tricks also.

If North lets go the ◇K or ◇Q on your ♠5 at trick 9, do not play a low diamond to knock out a diamond and set up your ◇J. A cunning North might have discarded down to ◇K-7, ♣K-9. It is safe and certain to play off your last spade to score ten tricks – and then chide partner for not bidding the game. (South could hold declarer to nine tricks with a club switch at trick 4, but this is easier in the *post mortem* than at the table.)

TIP 63:

Abandon the normal technique in handling a suit if you can tell that it will not work.

(1)
WEST	EAST	WEST	NORTH	EAST	SOUTH
♠ Q J 10 6 4	♠ A 7 5 3		No	No	No
♡ 8 6	♡ 10 4 3 2	1♠	2♡	3♡*	No
◇ K Q	◇ A 7	4♠	No	No	No
♣ A Q 5 4	♣ K 8 3	*Maximum pass with 4+ spades			

North leads the ♡K and ♡Q, South playing ♡9 and ♡5. North switches to the ♣10. How should West continue?

(2)
WEST	EAST	WEST	NORTH	EAST	SOUTH
♠ A J 10 7 3	♠ K 5 4 2				1♡
♡ 8 6	♡ 10 7	1♠	No	3♡*	No
◇ Q J 2	◇ A K 5 4	4♠	No	No	No
♣ K J 7	♣ Q 8 6	*Opening hand with 4+ spades			

North leads the ♡A and a low heart to South's ♡J. South plays the ♣A and a low club, won by West. How should West continue?

(1) The normal play in spades is to lead the queen and take the finesse. That play is sure to lose here. North's 2♡ bid will be based on five hearts and after the first two tricks, North's hearts must have been A-K-Q-J-7. North passed as dealer and cannot hold the ♠K as well. That would be 13 HCP and a 1♡ opening.

Play a spade to the ace and another spade. If South began with ♠K singleton, you have an overtrick. If South has ♠K-x or ♠K-x-x, you still make your contract. There is a risk in taking the spade finesse: South wins and if North ruffs the club return, you are one down.

(2) You have lost three tricks and cannot afford a trump loser. Normal technique is to cash the ♠K and ♠A and hope the ♠Q drops. However, South is marked with the ♠Q. You hold 12 HCP and so does dummy. North led the ♡A, leaving 12 HCP missing. As South opened in first seat, credit South with those points and hence the ♠Q. Play a spade to the king and a spade back. If South follows low, finesse the ♠J. A good bridge player never follows rules blindly.

TIP 64:

Do not play an honour if it cannot win the trick or cannot promote a winner for yourself or your partner.

The purpose of playing high cards is to win tricks or to build up winners. If a card cannot fulfil either of these functions, it is a waste to play it, unless you have some clear purpose in mind.

WEST	EAST	WEST	NORTH	EAST	SOUTH
♠ 8	♠ K 4 3 2			No	No
♡ A Q 8 6 5 4	♡ K J 9 2	1♡	No	3♡	No
◇ A 7 5	◇ K J 2	6♡	No	No	No
♣ A K 7	♣ 8 4	North leads ♠Q. Plan the play.			

The ♠Q lead marks South with the ♠A. Thus there is no point in playing the ♠K on the queen. It cannot win and it cannot build up a spade winner for you. To play the ♠K is futile, yet how often do we hear, 'I wanted to force out the ace'. Why? Forcing out the ace does you no good if it does not lead to an increase in your trick tally.

South may hold ♠ A 9 6 ♡ 7 ◇ Q 10 8 3 ♣ Q 10 6 5 2. If the ♠K is played at trick 1, West will take the diamond finesse later. One down. West should duck the spade lead, ruff a second low spade (sooner or later), draw trumps ending in dummy and play a third low spade, ruffing. If South has fewer than four spades, the ♠A will drop, leaving the ♠K high and the diamond finesse becomes unnecessary.

WEST	EAST	WEST	NORTH	EAST	SOUTH
♠ 7 2	♠ A 8 6 4		3♠	No	No
♡ A K Q 8 7 6 3	♡ J 10	4♡	No	No	No
◇ Q	◇ 8 5 4 2	North leads ♠K. Plan the play.			
♣ A 9 7	♣ K 8 4				

Did you play the ♠A on the ♠K? Oops. If so, you have missed the point of this tip: do not play an honour if it cannot win. The ♠A will be ruffed by South, of course, if North holds the seven spades expected for the 3♠ opening. Play low on the first spade and on the next spade, too, if North continues. If a third spade is led, play low in dummy and ruff in hand. The ♠A will still be there as your tenth trick later.

TIP 65:

To obtain a genuine count in a suit headed by the A-K-Q, lead the king, not the ace.

WEST	EAST	WEST	EAST
♠ A K Q 10	♠ 6 5 4	1NT	3NT
♡ K 8 6	♡ A 5 3	No	
◇ 9 8 7	◇ A K 6		
♣ 6 5 3	♣ A 7 4 2	North leads ♡Q. Plan the play.

Declarer has eight winners and needs four spade tricks for the contract. If the ♠J does not fall in the first two rounds, declarer will have to judge whether to finesse the ♠10 or play for the drop on the third round. The percentage play is for the jack to drop (see Tip 56) but you would like to make the winning decision at the table and not rely just on probabilities.

Competent defenders signal the count when declarer is tackling a suit (standard count is lowest with an odd number, high-low with an even number). If the opponents are avid and trustworthy count signallers, you can enlist their aid. If you play off ♠A and ♠K, you are advertising your strength and North might not signal length. If you take the lead in dummy and play low to the ♠K first, North may expect South to hold the ace and commence a high-low signal with a doubleton. If North completes a high-low signal when you continue with the ♠Q and North is not renowned for deceptive play, you have enough evidence to cross to dummy and finesse the ♠10. If North has given false count, you will know not to trust this North next time.

The same advice applies to this holding:

Dummy	Q 7 2	Lead the king from hand first rather
		than the ace and rather than low to
Declarer	A K 10 6	the queen first.

The king is more likely to give you true count from both opponents. If you obtain conflicting count signals, trust the signal from second player. Fourth player can often judge from partner's play what is happening and may give a fake count signal to try to mislead you.

TIP 66:

Pay very close attention to the bidding. You may be able to calculate the distribution of the cards very accurately if the opponents use off-beat methods to show unusual hand patterns.

Dealer North : East-West vulnerable

WEST	EAST	WEST	NORTH	EAST	SOUTH
♠ A	♠ K J 8 7	2♠*	Dble	3♣	
♡ J 10 8 5 4	♡ A K Q 3	3♡	5♣	6♡	All pass
◇ J 9 6 5	◇ A 7 2				
♣ K 9 3	♣ A 4				

*Unusual, two-suiter, both majors *OR* both minors, at least 5-5, 6-11 points

North leads the ♣Q. Plan the play.

Suppose you take the ♣A and play ♡A, ♡K, ♡Q. South follows and North discards two clubs on the second and third heart. How should West continue?

Suppose that West continues with the ♣K and a club ruff. South follows to the king but discards a low spade on the third club. What do you make of that? How would you continue?

Once you refer to the meaning of North's opening bid, the whole hand is a read-out. North began with six clubs (already known as South showed out on the third club) and 5+ diamonds (from the unusual 2♠ opening). That accounts for eleven of North's cards and as North followed to just one heart, the rest is easy. Play a spade to the ace and all is known. If North shows out of spades, the pattern will be 0-1-6-6 and if North follows, it will be 1-1-5-6. This was the complete deal:

Once North's pattern is known, it is easy to calculate South's. After drawing trumps and ruffing the third club, the remaining cards will be:

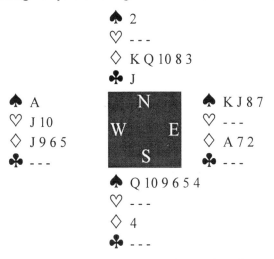

After a spade to the ace, play a diamond to the ace and South will have only spades left. Exit with the ♠8, allowing South to win as you discard a diamond. South must play a spade into dummy's K-J tenace, allowing you to discard your remaining diamond losers. Easy once you count North's cards.

TIP 67:

When trying to sneak a trick as declarer, lead the second card from a sequence in hand against a strong defender, but the bottom card from a sequence in hand against a weak defender.

Occasions abound where you wish to sneak a trick past a defender. In 3NT with a suit wide open, you want to snatch the ninth trick before the defenders realise where the weakness lies. Fearing a ruff in a trump contract, you want to lead two rounds of trumps and may wish to sneak one round of trumps from K-Q-J-10-5 opposite, say, 7-4-3-2. Leading the king will not work. Against a strong defender, the queen lead may cause second player to duck in case partner holds the king-singleton. Against a weak defender leading the ten will usually work, since the weak defender is conditioned to play second-hand-low and will hope partner can beat the ten.

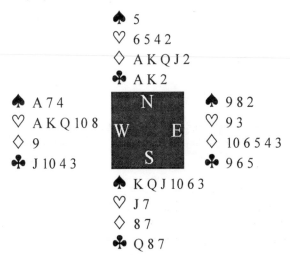

♠ 5
♡ 6 5 4 2
◊ A K Q J 2
♣ A K 2

♠ A 7 4   ♠ 9 8 2
♡ A K Q 10 8   ♡ 9 3
◊ 9   ◊ 10 6 5 4 3
♣ J 10 4 3   ♣ 9 6 5

♠ K Q J 10 6 3
♡ J 7
◊ 8 7
♣ Q 8 7

South is in 4♠ after West bid hearts. The defence can beat 4♠. After two top hearts, West leads a third heart, ruffed by East's ♠8 and over-ruffed by the ten. If West wins the top trump exit and plays another heart, East ruffs with ♠9, over-ruffed by South again. South is left with one top trump. When that is cashed, West's ♠7 will be high. One down. The defenders have executed a neat double uppercut.

Declarer cannot avoid this legitimately but can try to fool West into ducking the first round of trumps. After over-ruffing East's ♠8, try the ♠Q against a good defender, the ♠J against a poor defender. If West falls for it and plays low, the next top trump draws East's last trump, the second uppercut evaporates and West's ♠7 can be drawn safely.

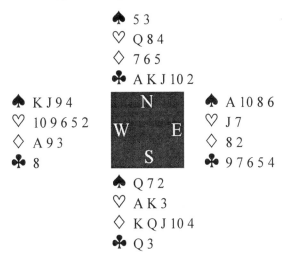

```
                    ♠ 5 3
                    ♡ Q 8 4
                    ◇ 7 6 5
                    ♣ A K J 10 2
  ♠ K J 9 4            N          ♠ A 10 8 6
  ♡ 10 9 6 5 2                     ♡ J 7
  ◇ A 9 3          W        E      ◇ 8 2
  ♣ 8                 S           ♣ 9 7 6 5 4
                    ♠ Q 7 2
                    ♡ A K 3
                    ◇ K Q J 10 4
                    ♣ Q 3
```

West leads the ♡5 against 3NT. With eight tricks available in hearts and clubs, South should try to sneak a diamond trick before the defenders realise the urgency to look for tricks in spades. It is a good idea here to play low in dummy and capture East's ♡J with the king. West may hope that East began with A-J-x over dummy's queen.

Now lead the ◇10 against weak opposition, the ◇Q against a good defender. Most weak defenders will duck the ◇10 and you have your ninth trick. Do not be greedy and try another diamond! Even if West takes the ◇A, most weak defenders will play another heart.

The ◇10 will not fool a strong West. When declarer leads an honour and you hold the card below it, this is a sure sign that declarer is trying to sneak a trick. Staring at the ◇9, West should see through your ruse, grab the ◇A to switch to the ♠4. Make your diamond play believable by leading the ◇Q and you may survive or you may not – a good defender did not become good by letting declarers steal contracts.

TIP 68:

Pay attention to the card chosen as the opening lead and make the most of the inferences given to you by that lead.

There is a wealth of information from the opening lead and a discerning declarer can draw valuable inferences in this area.

1. *How fast was the lead?* A defender with a naturally attractive lead will play at normal pace. When there is significant hesitation before the lead, declarer may deduce that the defender has no clear-cut lead and has some holdings which are unattractive.

2. *Was the choice a trump lead?* That normally indicates that trumps are splitting evenly. A trump lead is uncommon from four trumps – 'trump length, lead length': Tip 46.

3. *Is the lead in a suit bid by dummy or declarer?* If so, beware. That usually indicates a singleton lead.

WEST	EAST	WEST	EAST
♠ 8 7	♠ A Q 9 3 2	1♡	1♠
♡ A 8 7 6 4	♡ K 3 2	2◇	3♡
◇ A K Q 6	◇ 7 5	4♡	No
♣ K J	♣ Q 7 5	Lead: ♠4	Plan the play.

Finessing the ♠Q is an error you should not make twice. The likely upshot: South wins with the ♠K, gives North a spade ruff and a club to South's ace followed by another spade promotes a trump trick for the defence. Best is to rise with the ♠A and play ♡K, ♡A. As long as the trumps break you are home.

4. When the opening leader has bid a suit but does not lead it, if you and dummy have no high cards in the suit, the opening leader's suit is probably headed by the A-Q or just the ace.

5. When dummy has shown a longish suit and the lead is a trump, the defender on lead is likely to be strong in dummy's long suit. A good defender does not lead a trump if dummy's suit may run and provide declarer with several discards.

6. When declarer bids two suits and dummy gives a preference, a trump lead indicates that the leader is strong in declarer's other suit.

7. Against no-trumps, if the opening lead is from a 4-card suit, the leader will probably not hold greater length in any other unbid suit.

WEST	EAST	WEST	EAST
♠ 10 7 4	♠ A 9 5	1NT	3NT
♡ A K Q 10	♡ J 3 2	No	
◇ A 8 4	◇ K Q 10 7	Lead: ♠2. North discards a club
♣ 6 5 3	♣ Q J 8	on the second heart. Plan the play.

If North's ♠2 is fourth-highest, North began with four spades. North also has only one heart and so has eight cards in the minors. These figure to split 4-4, else North would probably have led from a 5-card suit. After you finish the hearts, play ◇K, diamond to the ace and a third diamond. If North follows to the third diamond and the ◇J has not yet appeared, finesse the ◇10. The diamond position is not a guess.

8. If a low card is led in a trump contract, assume that the leader does not hold the ace.

Dummy	K 6	If a low card against your trump contract, play dummy's 6, not the king. The ace will
Declarer	J 4	be on the right most of the time.

9. If you can tell that the lead is risky, such as leading an unsupported ace or from holdings like K-x-x, Q-x-x, J-x-x-x or similar, the leader probably has dangerous holdings in all suits.

10. If the lead is very unusual, see what follows.

Dummy	♡ J 6	You are in 4♠ after LHO opened 3♡. The lead is the ♡2. What do you make of that?
Declarer	♡ 7 4	

The ♡2 cannot be a true card (cannot be fourth-highest from a 7-card suit). A wildly abnormal lead is used as a suit-preference signal – in the case of a pre-empt, it usually indicates a void. The ♡2 suggests that LHO is void in clubs. Play the ♡J from dummy just in case LHO was desperate enough to lead the ♡2 from A-K-Q-x-x-x-x in the hope of finding partner with the ♡J.

TIP 69:

When playing K-Q-10 in hand opposite low cards in dummy, play low to the queen first, *not the king*, to tempt the defender with the ace sitting over you to take the ace and spare you the guess on the next round.

(1)	8 4 3		(2)	8 4 3	
A 9 5		J 7 6 2	J 7 6 2		A 9 5
	K Q 10			K Q 10	

If you know the location of the ace or the jack and you have sufficient entries, you can always play K-Q-10 for two tricks (unless there is A-J-x or longer offside). The problem is that you usually play low to the king, which holds, cross to dummy and lead low. When second player follows low on the second round, you have to decide whether to finesse the 10 (wins in layout 1, loses in 2) or whether to rise with the queen (loses in 1, wins in 2).

Because declarer is unlikely to lead to an unsupported king if anything else is offering, a defender generally knows that if a low card is led from dummy to declarer's king, declarer usually has more than just the king. Consequently, good defenders can usually duck smoothly in situation 1, leaving you with a nasty guess on the second round of the suit.

You can frequently catch a defender out by leading low to your *queen*. Firstly, they may now expect that partner holds the king and will not wish to duck. If the ace captures the queen, you can finesse the ten later. Secondly, caught unawares by the queen rather than the expected king, they might not duck smoothly. Perhaps you can diagnose a defender's dilemma even if they do eventually duck. If you place the ace with LHO, you would again cross to dummy in another suit and finesse the 10 next.

TIP 70:

If possible, play your suit combinations to prevent the defenders signalling. If a trick is sure to be lost when you are setting up a long suit or drawing trumps, lose it early to minimise the opportunity for the defenders to signal.

WEST	EAST	WEST	EAST
♠ A K	♠ Q 9 4	1◇	2◇
♡ Q 6	♡ 5 4 2	3NT	No
◇ A 8 6 4 3	◇ 10 9 7 5 2	Lead: ♣J. South plays the ♣5.
♣ K Q 6 2	♣ A 7	How should West plan the play?

With seven top tricks, West must play on diamonds but that involves losing the lead. If the defence then finds the heart switch, it is curtains. Some macho declarers might take the ♣A and lead a heart, attacking the weak holding in the hope that the defenders will abandon any thoughts of attacking in that area.

You do not need to resort to such desperation here. Your best shot is: (1) Take the ♣A and play the ♣6 from hand. If you win in hand, your club strength is revealed. If you follow with the ♣2, North might be able to read South's ♣5 as discouraging. By concealing the ♣2, you may persuade North that South is encouraging from ♣Q-5-2.

(2) Play a diamond and duck it, hoping that North wins the trick. It may be too hard for North to find the heart switch. A defender who did not find the killing lead is unlikely to find the killing switch without any signal from partner. If you take the ◇A and play another diamond, if North wins this, South can signal for a switch to hearts. Ducking the first diamond may prevent South's signal.

Ducking the diamond is also important if North has the ◇K bare (or the ◇Q bare if South followed with the ◇J). Otherwise, ◇A and another diamond allows South on lead and South is more likely to switch to hearts. When giving up the lead, try to give it to the defender who is unlikely to know the position, not to the one who probably does know it. If possible, lose the lead to the weaker defender, not to the stronger.

TIP 71:

After an opponent's pre-empt, play for any critical card in the other suits to be with the partner of the pre-emptor.

WEST	EAST	WEST	NORTH	EAST	SOUTH
♠ K 5 2	♠ A 8 7 4 3		3◇	Dble*	No
♡ K 10 9 3 2	♡ A J 5 4	4♡	No	No	No
◇ Q 4	◇ 7 2	*For takeout			
♣ K J 3	♣ A Q				

North leads the ◇J to South's ◇A and wins the diamond return. North shifts to the ♣7. How would you plan the play?

With no opposition bidding, you play the hearts in the normal way, ace and king and hope the ♡Q drops. After the pre-empt the odds favour playing the pre-emptor to be short in your long suit. ♡Q-x-x with South is more likely than ♡Q-x with North. Therefore play the ♡A and finesse against South on the next round. Likewise, if South had opened 3◇, you would cash ♡K and then finesse against North.

WEST	EAST	WEST	NORTH	EAST	SOUTH
♠ K J 9 7 2	♠ A 10 5 3		3♣	Dble*	No
♡ 8	♡ K Q J 4	4♠	No	No	No
◇ K J 8 3	◇ A Q 9	*For takeout			
♣ J 7 2	♣ 8 3				

North leads the ♣K, taken by South with the ace. A heart goes to North's ace and North continues with the ♣Q, on which South discards a diamond. North plays the ♣10 next. How would you play?

Given North's 3♣ opening you tend to place the ♠Q with South. So far North has shown up with ♣K-Q and ♡A, 9 HCP. It is wildly unlikely that North has the ♠Q as well. Do not discard on the third club or ruff it low in dummy. South's over-ruff will defeat you. Rise with the ♠A and then lead the ♠10, running it if South plays low. If the ♠10 holds, repeat the spade finesse as often as necessary. You can even deal with South's holding ♠Q-8-6-4.

TIP 72:

Do not follow any tip blindly. Do not settle for probabilities if you can discover the location of vital cards with certainty. You may be able to force the opponents to reveal what they hold.

WEST	EAST	WEST	NORTH	EAST	SOUTH
♠ K 10 8 6 2	♠ A Q 9 3		3♡	Dble*	4♡
♡ 8 7	♡ J 10	4♠	No	No	No
◇ 9	◇ K Q 8	*For takeout			
♣ K 10 9 7 4	♣ A J 6 3				

North leads the ♡K and the second heart is won by South's ace. South shifts to the ♠4, won by dummy's ♠9, North playing ♠5. You play ♠A and a spade to your king, South following with ♠7 and ♠J, while North discards two hearts. How would you continue?

Suppose you play the ◇9 to dummy's king and South's ◇A. South returns a diamond, dummy's queen capturing North's ◇J. What next?

Having drawn trumps, you may be tempted to tackle clubs and, following Tip 71, place the ♣Q with South, so that ♣A and a club to the ten is indicated. Even after a diamond to the king and ace and a diamond return from South, you may be eager to start on the clubs.

Resist that urge. There is not the same urgency to broach a side suit as there would be if that suit were trumps. You might discover more information by playing the other suits first. It costs you nothing to ruff dummy's third diamond first and see what happens.

Suppose that North discards another heart when you ruff the third diamond. You now know that North started with *one* spade and *two* diamonds precisely. Give North *seven* hearts for the 3♡ opening and you know ten of North's cards. That means North must hold *three* clubs. Now the club play has become a sure thing: cash the ♣K and lead the ♣10, finessing against North, a play you would not have produced had you followed Tip 71 blindly. North's hand:

♠ 5   ♡ K Q 9 6 4 3 2   ◇ J 7   ♣ Q 8 2

111

TIP 73:

Even though standard technique may be to take a finesse, beware of the normal finesse play in trumps if a ruff is threatening.

WEST	EAST	WEST	NORTH	EAST	SOUTH
♠ K J 5	♠ 10 6 4 3	1♡	Dble	2♡	No
♡ Q J 10 9 4	♡ A 6 3 2	4♡	No	No	No
◇ A	◇ 8 6				
♣ A Q 9 3	♣ K 8 7	North leads ◇K. Plan West's play.

It looks so easy. Take the ◇A and lead the ♡Q for a finesse. Even if the finesse loses, you will not lose more than one heart and two spades at worst, will you?

Just wait a minute! Reflect on the bidding for a moment. North doubled and so is likely to hold the ♡K but if not, North should have all the other significant high cards including the A-Q in spades. In addition, the takeout double means North is likely to hold four spades. That would leave South with just two spades. Now the danger in taking the heart finesse has become clear.

You can foresee what is likely to happen if South has something like:

♠ 9 2   ♡ K 8   ◇ 9 7 5 4 3 2   ♣ 6 5 4

South captures your ♡Q and switches to the ♠9. After North takes ♠Q and ♠A, the third spade gives South a ruff. One down.

The best move after taking the ◇A is to lead the ♡Q, tempting North to cover if holding the king. *Lead the top of equal honours if you want a defender to cover your honour.* If North plays low on the ♡Q, do not let the queen run – you were never intending to take the finesse. Rise with the ♡A and play a second heart. This will draw trumps if they are 2-2 and you escape the spade ruff. You may lose to the ♡K but that does not cost the contract. It is the spade ruff that could lay you low.

If South started with ♡K-x-x, you have no way of escaping the spade ruff if it exists, but you do not need to fail if South has just ♡K-x.

TIP 74:

Form a habit of counting your obvious winners even in a trump contract. This will often indicate what is needed for success.

WEST	EAST	WEST	NORTH	EAST	SOUTH
♠ 2	♠ 8 7 6 4 3	3♡	No	4♡	No
♡ K Q J 9 6 4 3	♡ A 10 8	No	No		
◇ 8 2	◇ A 9				
♣ 9 6 3	♣ A 5 4	Lead: ♣Q. Plan West's play.			

Many players would win with the ♣A and start on trumps, ending one off and venting their spleen on partner later for 'that skimpy raise'. Such a statement could rebound if partner can retort correctly, 'You could have made it.'

Most textbooks recommend counting your losers in trump contracts. This is sensible but it does not hurt to count also your sure winners, especially when they are obvious. You have seven hearts tricks and two aces. Where can you find a tenth trick? There are no ruffs in dummy, no extra high cards to establish. The only hope lies in the spade suit. You have to hope the spades are 4-3. If so, you can set up the fifth spade for a diamond discard.

The timing is important. Take the ♣A and play a spade at once. You need all those hearts in dummy as entries to ruff spades and to reach the fifth spade at the end of the day.

On taking the spade, the opponents will probably cash two rounds of clubs and then shift to a diamond. Take the ◇A, ruff a spade, play a heart to the ♡8, ruff a spade, cross to the ♡10 and ruff another spade. If the spades were 4-3, dummy's last spade is now high. Play a heart to the ace, cash the fifth spade and away goes the diamond loser.

Note that even one round of trumps before conceding the spade would have been fatal. You would be one entry short.

TIP 75:

If one opponent is marked with shortage in one suit, place that opponent with length in another critical suit. If you are missing an honour card in the critical suit, play the opponent known or expected to have length in that suit to hold the missing honour.

WEST	EAST				
♠ 5 3	♠ 10 7				
♡ K 9 6 5	♡ A 2				
◇ A Q 9 5	◇ K 10 3 2				
♣ 8 6 2	♣ Q 10 9 5 3				

Dealer East : North-South vulnerable

WEST	NORTH	EAST	SOUTH
		No	1♣
No	1♠	No	2♠
No	No	2NT*	No
3◇	No	No	No

*Delayed takeout, both minors
(see Tip 25)

North leads the ♣J, queen, king. South cashes the ♣A, North discarding a spade, and continues with the ♣7, ruffed by North, who switches to the ♠K. South follows with the ♠9, encouraging, and North plays a low spade to South's ace. South plays the ♣4. What would you play on that?

You are already one off, but that is the price for competing against their unassailable 2♠. There is no need to go two off if you can avoid it.

Should you ruff high or with the ◇9? This is where Tip 75 can help. North is known to be short in clubs and so is likely to have more diamonds than South. Placing the ◇J with the player with greater length means that you assume North has the ◇J. In that case if you ruff with the ◇9, North will over-ruff with the ◇J.

Take the hint, ruff with the ◇A and then start on the trumps with ◇Q and a second diamond. If North began with ◇J-x-x, the ◇J will appear on the second round of trumps and the rest are yours.

If North follows low on the second round of diamonds, the better shot is to play the ◇K and assume North started with ◇x-x-x and South with ◇J-x. This is more likely than North starting with ◇J-x-x-x. With a singleton, South might have pushed on to 3♠ and with four trumps and a singleton in partner's suit, North might have doubled 3◇.

TIP 76:

Be prepared to re-assess your plan of play if a surprising development occurs.

WEST	EAST	WEST	NORTH	EAST	SOUTH
♠ A K J 3 2	♠ 8 5 4	2♣	No	2◇	No
♡ A K 4 3	♡ Q 8 2	2♠	No	3♠	No
◇ 6 3	◇ A 5	4♣*	No	4◇*	No
♣ A K	♣ 8 7 4 3 2	6♠	No	No	No

*Cue-bid

Lead: ◇K. Plan West's play.

West's jump to 6♠ was a little impetuous. We have all been in better slams but also in worse. There is no value in worrying about the bidding once the lead is made. Focus on bringing your contract home.

You might think along these lines: 'All will be well if trumps are 3-2 with the ♠Q onside and hearts are 3-3. In that case, I do not need the ♠Q onside, I can play ♠A, ♠K, cash the hearts and pitch the diamond from dummy on the thirteenth heart. The ♠Q may ruff this but I can ruff my diamond loser with dummy's last trump.'

A trump is led from dummy and South plays the ♠Q! This could be a falsecard from ♠Q-x but that could be very silly if West's trumps were A-J-10-x-x-x. Treat the ♠Q as genuine and so a singleton.

In that case you must re-assess your plan. It will not do to play ♠A, ♠K and run the hearts. Even though you are lucky to find them 3-3, North would ruff the thirteenth heart and lead the last trump. That removes dummy's last trump and leaves you with a diamond loser.

Capture the ♠Q and do not play a second trump. Tackle the hearts next. You need them to be 3-3. When that transpires, play the thirteenth heart and discard dummy's diamond. North may ruff this but you can win any return, ruff your diamond loser, come to hand and draw North's trumps. Successful players are flexible declarers.

TIP 77:

If there is only one lie of the cards which will allow your contract to succeed, assume the cards lie that way.

WEST	EAST	WEST	NORTH	EAST	SOUTH
♠ 4 3	♠ Q 8 6 5			1♣	1♠
♡ J 8 6 4 2	♡ K 10 5 3	2♡	No	4♡	No
◇ K Q J 8	◇ A	No	No		
♣ K 2	♣ A Q 9 4	Lead: ♠K			

South encourages with the ♠9 and North continues with the ♠2. You play low in dummy and South wins with the ♠10. South now plays the ♠7. What should West do?

As South figures to have five spades for the 1♠ overcall, North will be out of spades. This is confirmed by North's ♠K lead. There is only one layout of the trump suit which will allow you to succeed. Once you deduce what that is you will ruff with the ♡J. This wins the trick, North discarding a diamond. How should West proceed?

If North was unable to over-ruff the ♡J, South will have ♡A-Q. Then you are doomed, no matter what. Forget that possibility – successful players are always optimists.

What position allows you to succeed? North cannot have the ♡A-Q. With that North would have over-ruffed to ensure one down. In fact, North cannot hold the ♡Q at all, else North would have over-ruffed your ♡J. The only hope is that North has the ♡A and South the ♡Q.

Therefore you lead a heart at trick 4, ♡7 from North, and you play the ♡K from dummy. Sure enough, South's ♡Q drops and you concede just one trump trick to North (cross to hand with a club and lead a heart towards dummy). North began with:

♠ K 2   ♡ A 9 7   ◇ 10 9 6 4 2   ♣ 8 6 3

Note that North did well not to over-ruff your ♡J with the ace. Otherwise the location of the ♡Q would be transparent and the need to play the ♡K to drop the ♡Q singleton would be even more obvious.

TIP 78:

Assume that a competent opponent will not commit an elementary blunder.

WEST	EAST	WEST	NORTH	EAST	SOUTH
♠ K Q J 3 2	♠ A 10 8 6	1♠	No	3♣	No
♡ K 10 9 7	♡ A 6 3	3♡	No	3♠	No
◇ A 10	◇ K 2	4♠	No	4NT	No
♣ 8 5	♣ A Q 10 6	5♠*	No	6♠	All pass

*Two key cards plus the ♠Q

North leads the ◇3. Plan the play. South has ♠9-5-4, North the ♠7.

A heart loser is almost certain and 6♠ seems to hinge on the club finesse. A thought may cross your mind to play ♡A, ♡K and a third heart after drawing trumps and cashing the second diamond. If South has ♡Q-J-x or fails to unblock with ♡Q-x-x, the third heart will endplay South. This avoids the need for the club finesse. If North has ♡Q-x-x or ♡Q-J-x, you can always fall back on the club finesse.

The fallacy is that a competent South would see the endplay looming and would jettison the ♡Q from Q-x-x and even the ♡Q and ♡J from Q-J-x. That would free South from any endplay. Another flaw is that the hearts may not be 3-3 anyway.

In fact, North held:

♠ 7   ♡ Q J 8 2   ◇ Q 7 4 3   ♣ K 4 3 2

When declarer did adopt the attempted end-play (◇A, three rounds of spades, ◇K, ♡A, ♡K and a third heart), North won and played the fourth heart. Forced to ruff, declarer was stranded in dummy to lead away from ♣A-Q-10-6.

Recommended is to win the lead, draw trumps ending in West and finesse the ♣Q. If this wins it is all over. If South has the ♣K, declarer can win any return in dummy and play for a club-heart squeeze. If North has the hand above but with ♣J-x-x-x, North cannot guard both hearts and clubs and will succumb to the squeeze.

TIP 79:

With suits like K-Q-J-x opposite A-10-x-x, you can choose the order in which the winners are played. You can thus force the opponent shorter in this suit to make two or more discards before receiving a useful signal from partner.

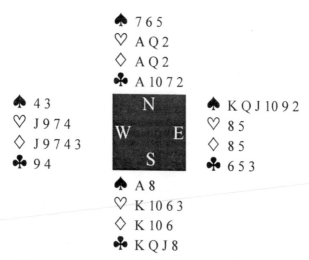

South is 6NT after a weak 2♠ opening by East. West leads the ♠4 and South wins the second spade. Success hinges on declarer's making four heart tricks. West can prevent that but does not know South's exact pattern. South could just as easily hold four diamonds and three hearts.

South plays the clubs to give West the discarding problem: club to the ace, club back to the king, ♣Q and ♣J. On the third club West will discard a diamond but on the fourth club West must discard with J-x-x-x in each suit. If West knew South's 4-card red suit, West would know which suit to keep and which to ditch. As West does not know, West will guess wrongly some of the time.

If South were to play ♣K, ♣Q, club to dummy and lead the fourth club from dummy, East could play either red eight to show a doubleton. That would be enough for West to work out the red suit position and discard a diamond.

TIP 80:

When you have a choice of ways to play a key suit, do not commit yourself until you have studied all the inferences from the bidding, the opening lead and the play so far.

	Dealer East : N-S vulnerable	WEST	NORTH	EAST	SOUTH
WEST	EAST			No	1♣
♠ A Q 6 4	♠ 9 5 3	1◇	1♡	No	1NT*
♡ 3	♡ 10 8 6 2	3◇	3NT	No	No
◇ Q 10 9 8 6 4 3	◇ A	4◇	Dble	All pass	
♣ A	♣ J 8 7 6 2	*15-17 points			

North leads the ♣Q. Plan West's play.

The 4◇ sacrifice has turned out badly but if you make 4◇ doubled, there will be no recriminations. Success forgives all errors.

You take the ♣A, cross to the ◇A (North plays ◇2, South ◇7) and finesse the ♠Q which holds. How do you continue?

You have to lose a heart, a spade and a diamond. To make 4◇ doubled, you cannot afford two diamond losers. You must hope that the ◇K and ◇J are split, either ◇J-x opposite ◇K-x-x (lead the queen to pin the jack) or ◇J-x-x opposite ◇K-x (lead low, dropping the king, and capture the jack later). Which situation exists?

When facing this kind of problem, review the data thus far and try to reconstruct the opponents' hands, suit by suit:

Spades: To succeed, you need spades 3-3. Assume that is the case.

Hearts: South will not hold four hearts (would have raised) and North will not have six hearts (would have rebid 3♡ or 4♡ and not 3NT). Thus North should have five hearts and South three.

Clubs: North led the ♣Q. With the ♣J in dummy, this indicates North began with ♣Q-x. That gives South five clubs.

North's pattern can be deduced to be 3-5-3-2 and South has 3-3-2-5. The ◇K will be with South for the 1NT rebid and so the winning move is a low diamond at trick 4. South held:

♠ K J 2   ♡ K Q 4   ◇ K 7   ♣ K 10 5 4 3

TIPS 81-100: Defensive strategy

TIP 81:

Keep track of the tricks needed to defeat the contract.

Do not pursue a line of defence with no chance of success. Make a conscious mental note of the tricks you need to beat declarer and you will frequently find the right path and avoid futile plays, doomed to failure.

(1)

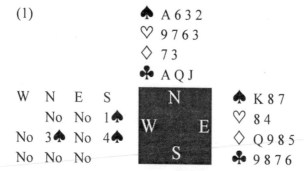

```
               ♠ A 6 3 2
               ♡ 9 7 6 3
               ◇ 7 3
               ♣ A Q J
W   N   E   S        N          ♠ K 8 7
    No  No  1♠                  ♡ 8 4
No  3♣  No  4♠    W       E     ◇ Q 9 8 5
No  No  No           S         ♣ 9 8 7 6
```

West leads ◇4: three, queen, ace. South plays ♠Q: nine, two, king. How should East continue?

(2)

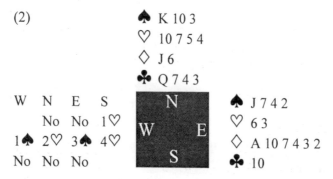

```
               ♠ K 10 3
               ♡ 10 7 5 4
               ◇ J 6
               ♣ Q 7 4 3
W   N   E   S        N          ♠ J 7 4 2
    No  No  1♡                  ♡ 6 3
1♠  2♡  3♠  4♡    W       E     ◇ A 10 7 4 3 2
No  No  No           S         ♣ 10
```

West leads ◇5: six, ace, eight. How should East continue?

Solutions: (1) It is a sound guide to return partner's lead in general, but check whether that can produce the tricks needed to beat the contract.

If dummy were void in diamonds, you would not consider bringing a diamond back. With a singleton left in dummy, a diamond return is just as futile here. The ♠K is one trick and you can score at most one trick from diamonds. Where can you find two more tricks? Clearly not in clubs and so it has to be from the hearts. East should switch to the ♡8. If West has ♡A-Q-x-x / ◇J-x-x-x-x, East will score a heart ruff and defeat 4♠, while a diamond return can let the game make.

Suppose West holds: ♠ 9   ♡ K Q 5 2   ◇ K 10 6 4 2   ♣ 10 4 2

and so South has: ♠ Q J 10 5 4   ♡ A J 10   ◇ A J   ♣ K 5 3

Now the heart return is also vital to prevent a later endplay on West. If East plays back a diamond, West would win but cannot afford to play a heart. West could exit safely only with a club. South would win, draw trumps, eliminate clubs and lead a heart to the ten, endplaying West. On a heart return at trick 2, ducked, West can win with the ♡Q, cash the ◇K and exit with a club. West will then come to the ♡K in due course.

(2) It is encouraging to all of us that in the 1981 World Championships East muffed the defence when he took the ◇A and returned a diamond. Had East paid attention to the tricks needed to defeat 4♡, the futility of the diamond return would have been recognised.

Four tricks are needed. The ◇A is one and at most there will be one spade trick and one more diamond trick. If there is no trump trick, a club trick is vital and East should shift to the ♣10 at trick 2.

As it happened the club switch would defeat 4♡ by two tricks, as West held:

   ♠ A Q 9 8 5   ♡ Q 2   ◇ Q 9 5   ♣ A 9 2

The successful defence goes club to the ace, ♣9 ruffed, spade to the ace, club ruff. Two down. On the actual diamond return at trick 2, South won with the king and drew trumps. South held:

   ♠ 6   ♡ A K J 9 8   ◇ K 8   ♣ K J 8 6 5

East-West have a sacrifice available (4♠ doubled is one off) but why sacrifice when you can defeat their game by competent defence?

TIP 82:

Stop and count the cards in a suit after two rounds have gone.

After two rounds of a suit have been played you can frequently tell what is happening in that suit. Note the order in which partner played the cards and you will have a picture of what is happening in the suit after you take into account dummy's holding and your own cards.

West leads ♡8: five, queen, nine. On the ♡K, South plays the ♡J and West the ♡7. How should East continue?

In many club games East would play the ♡A at trick 3. West would discard a club or a diamond and 3♠ would make easily if the missing hands look like this:

West :   ♠ 9 8   ♡ 8 7   ◇ J 9 6 5 4 3   ♣ 10 9 8

South: ♠ A K Q 10 6   ♡ J 9 4   ◇ 10 8 2   ♣ 7 6

Three hearts and one diamond will not beat the contract. East needs two diamond tricks. If East has counted the hearts after two rounds, the solution is easy: From West's ♡8 – ♡7, East knows West started with two hearts and South with three. East now leads a low heart for West to ruff and West makes the obvious diamond return. One off.

It is true that West should ruff the ♡A at trick 3 and switch to diamonds anyway, but remember the First Law of Defence: If you give partner the chance to do the wrong thing, partner grabs that chance.

TIP 83:

A high card from partner when playing third-hand-high denies the card immediately below it.

A general principle for defenders is to win a trick as cheaply as possible. A corollary of this rule is that when playing third-hand-high, you play the cheapest of equally high cards. In many cases this makes it easy for partner to deduce the cards held by you and by declarer.

If third-hand-high plays the cheapest of equally high cards, it follows that the card played by third hand denies the card immediately below it. Otherwise that would be an equal and cheaper card.

NORTH 7 5 WEST J 8 6 4 2	West leads the 4 and East plays the 10, taken by the ace. West can tell that South started with A-K-Q-9. Holding the K or Q, East would have played it as third-hand-high.

South must hold the 9 as well as the A-K-Q, as East's 10 denies the 9. With 10-9, East should play the 9. If West leads the suit again, a trick is lost. Also West cannot afford to discard two cards in this suit.

NORTH 7 5 3 WEST Q 8 6 4 2	West leads the 4 and East plays the 10, taken by South with the ace. What is the exact layout of this suit?

East cannot have the K (would have played it third-hand-high). South does not have the jack (would have captured the 10 with the jack. East's 10 denies the 9. Therefore South will hold A-K-9, East has J-10 and it is safe for West to lead the suit again.

NORTH 7 5 3 WEST K 9 6 4 2	West leads the 4. If East plays the jack and South wins with the ace, West knows that East has the queen and South has the 10. It is safe to continue the suit.

Had East played the queen, taken by South, West knows that South has the jack (denied by the queen). It would be an error for West to lead a low card in this suit later. Play the king or try to find partner's entry.

TIP 84:

Do not play third-hand-high if it will benefit only declarer.

In a trump contract partner should not lead a low card at trick one if holding the ace in the suit led. Knowing declarer holds the ace may enable third player to calculate that third-hand-high cannot win the trick and will build up winners only for declarer or dummy. There is no merit in playing a high card if the only beneficiary is declarer.

(1)   NORTH   Dummy plays the jack on West's 5.
             K J 10 9 8   What should East do?
                     EAST
Lead: 5   Q 7 6 3 2

(2)   NORTH   Dummy plays the queen on West's 8.
             Q J 10 7   What should East do?
                     EAST
Lead: 8   K 6 4 3

(3)   NORTH   Dummy plays the ten on West's 8.
             K 10 9 6 3   What should East do?
                     EAST
Lead: 8   J 5 4 2

(1) The situation could be either of these:

```
        NORTH              OR          NORTH
        K J 10 9 8                     K J 10 9 8
WEST          EAST             WEST          EAST
5             Q 7 6 3 2        5 4           Q 7 6 3 2
        SOUTH                          SOUTH
        A 4                            A
```

If East plays the queen, South has five tricks whichever position exists. If East correctly plays low, declarer can score four tricks at most.

(2) South might have A-9-2 or A-2. If East plays the king, South has four tricks. If East plays low, South has three tricks.

(3) If South has A-Q and East plays the jack, South has five tricks. Playing low holds South to four tricks. With A-Q-7, South always has five tricks once West led the 8. East's playing low blocks the suit.

124

TIP 85:

Do not cover an honour with an honour if partner is expected to be short in the suit and you have no clear-cut card to be promoted.

The purpose of covering an honour is to win the trick or build up a trick for your side. If that is not possible, do not cover the honour. If you have no card to promote by covering, then to cover will help only if partner has a significant, promotable card. If partner has at most two cards in the suit, then that possibility is almost non-existent.

	NORTH	
	Q 6 4 2	
		EAST
		K 7 5

If this is the trump suit and the queen is led from dummy, should East cover? East has no secondary card to promote and West figures to have only one or two cards. As it can almost never gain to cover, East should play low.

Can it cost to cover? You'd better believe it.

	Q 6 4 2	
A		K 7 5
	J 10 9 8 3	

If this is the layout, South will be chortling if you cover and so telescope two tricks into one.

Some wrongly argue that they are hoping to promote partner's jack. If partner does have the jack you will make one trick anyway.

	Q 6 4 2	
J 8		K 7 5
	A 10 9 3	

If East covers, West's jack scores later, but if East plays low, the defence still makes one trick.

	J 7 5 4 2	
K		Q 6
	A 10 9 8 3	

If East covers the jack, declarer has no loser. If East plays low, the defence scores one trick.

If partner cannot have two cards in the suit, it can be expensive to cover even if you do have some cards to promote.

	J 6	
K		Q 10 9 2
	A 8 7 5 4 3	

South opened a weak two in this suit and leads the jack from dummy to cater for bare 9 or 10 with West.

If East covers, South loses two tricks. If East plays low, South has three losers.

TIP 86:

Third hand plays the lower honour when holding a 'near-surround' combination over dummy's honour.

Third-hand-high is vital when dummy has nothing but low cards. With an honour card in dummy, that situation may change.

West leads the 4.

Dummy plays low.

(1) NORTH		(2) NORTH	
Q 6 5		10 7 5	
	EAST		EAST
	K J 3		J 9 3

These are obvious. (1) East plays the jack. (2) East plays the 9. In each case East has a perfect surround of dummy's honour. A 'near-surround' exists when the higher or lower card with East is one or two cards away from the perfect surround. In each of these examples, West leads the 4 and dummy plays low. What should East play?

(3) NORTH		(4) NORTH		(5) NORTH	
K 6 5		K 6 5		K 6 5	
	EAST		EAST		EAST
	A J 3		A 10 3		A 8 3

(3) Play the jack, not the ace.

(4) It is usually best to play the ten and keep the ace to capture the king.

(5) Play the ace. The 8 here is too low to create a near-surround.

(6) NORTH		(7) NORTH		(8) NORTH	
Q 6 5		Q 6 5		Q 6 5	
	EAST		EAST		EAST
	A J 3		K 10 3		A J 10

(6) Play the jack, not the ace.

(7) Play the 10, not the king.

(8) Play the 10, lower of equal cards in third seat (Tip 83).

(9) NORTH		(10) NORTH		(11) NORTH	
A J 5		A J 5		A 10 5	
	EAST		EAST		EAST
	K 10 3		Q 9 3		Q 9 3

(9) It is usually better to play the 10, not the king.

(10) It is usually better to play the 9, not the queen.

(11) It is usually better to play the 9, not the queen.

TIP 87:

Lead top of the 'imaginary sequence' when you sit over dummy and a surround position exists.

Consider these positions:

```
(1)   J 6 5           (2)   10 4 3          (3)   10 4 3
8 7 4      A Q 10 3   7 6 2       K J 9 8   A 7 6       K J 9 8
      K 9 2                 A Q 5                 Q 5 2
```

(1) If East plays the 3 or the ace-then-3, declarer has two tricks by playing low. If East leads the queen, South's king winning, and East waits for West to lead the suit next, South makes just one trick.

(2) If East leads the 8 or 9, declarer has three tricks by playing low and letting the 10 win. If East leads the jack, declarer can be held to two tricks if East waits for West to lead the suit next.

(3) If East leads the 8 or 9, declarer makes one trick by playing low. If East leads the jack, declarer makes no tricks.

The common features of these positions are:
(a) The defender is sitting over dummy, *and*
(b) The defender has dummy's high card surrounded, *and*
(c) The defender has another higher, non-touching honour: the ace in (1) and the king in (2) and (3).

In these cases, imagine dummy's surrounded card is in the defender's hand and make the standard lead from that holding. Thus, in (1) East imagines holding A-Q-J-10-3 and leads the queen, while in (2) and (3) East visualises K-J-10-9-8 and leads the jack.

What should East lead in these positions if about to attack this suit?

```
(4)   9 7 4           (5)   9 7 4           (6)   A 9 4
5 3        Q 10 8 6   K 5 3       Q 10 8 6  K 5 3       Q 10 8 6
      A K J 2               A J 2                 J 7 2
```

East has dummy's 9 surrounded in each case. Visualising the 9 in hand gives you Q-10-9-8-6 and so lead the 10 each time. This holds South to three tricks in (4) and to one trick in (5) and (6). A low card from East allows South to play low and score an extra trick each time.

TIP 88:

If partner plays cards in an abnormal order, partner is sending you a message, usually a suit-preference signal.

♠ A 9 6 3   ♡ K J 5   ◇ 9 5 2   ♣ 10 6 5

♠ 8	N	W	N	E	S
♡ A 8 6 4 3	W E				1♠
◇ J 10 7 6 3	S	No	2♠	No	4♠
♣ J 2		No	No	No	

West leads the ◇6, East winning with the ace. East continues with the ◇K. What should West play on that?

East's play in diamonds should make an impact on West. A defender wins as cheaply as possible but East played ◇A-then-◇K. The message is that East has ◇A-K doubleton and needs to know West's entry. West should play the ◇J under the ◇K, asking East to switch to hearts. When the problem is entry location, high card asks for the high suit, lowest card asks for the low suit, trumps excluded.

♠ A K 8 2   ♡ Q J 5 3   ◇ 9 5 2   ♣ K 9

♠ 9 7 6 5 3	N	W	N	E	S
♡ 9 2	W E			1◇	Dble
◇ 8 6		No	2◇	No	2♡
♣ 8 6 5 4	S	No	4♡	All pass	

West leads the ◇8, East winning with the ace. East continues with the ◇K and then the ◇4, South following ◇7, ◇10, ◇J. What should West play after ruffing the third diamond?

Again East has made an abnormal play in diamonds by playing the ace first. This is a request for you to play the high suit when you ruff. West should switch to a spade. This allows East to ruff, as East has:

♠ - - -   ♡ 8 7 6   ◇ A K Q 4 3   ♣ Q J 7 3 2

Without the spade ruff, the defence cannot defeat 4♡.

TIP 89:

If partner starts discarding from the suit led initially, this normally means you should not return the suit.

Having found a good lead, partner will want the suit returned and would not discard from that suit. If partner has found a poor lead, partner will start discarding from that suit to warn you against playing it back. Particularly at no-trumps, one tends not to discard from a suit you wish partner to play.

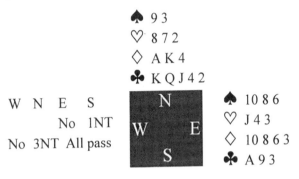

```
                  ♠ 9 3
                  ♡ 8 7 2
                  ◇ A K 4
                  ♣ K Q J 4 2
W  N  E  S        N           ♠ 10 8 6
      No 1NT                  ♡ J 4 3
                  W       E
No 3NT All pass              ◇ 10 8 6 3
                  S          ♣ A 9 3
```

West leads the ♠4, nine, ten, king. South leads the ♣10, seven, two . . .? Plan East's defence.

East should duck this club and also the next club, on which West plays the ♣5, and win the third club. What should East return?

East ducks the first two clubs, not to cut declarer off from dummy – impossible here – but to obtain a signal from partner. If West throws a discouraging heart, East will return the ♠8, defeating 3NT if West began with, say, ♠ A J 5 4 2 ♡ Q 9 5 ◇ J 7 5 ♣ 7 5.

On the other hand, West might have led from a poor spade suit:

♠ J 7 5 4 2 ♡ A Q 10 5 ◇ J 7 ♣ 7 5

If West discards a spade, preferably the ♠J from this hand, East should switch to hearts, choosing the ♡J, not the standard low one. As four heart tricks are needed, the ♡J is necessary. If East leads a low heart, South can duck and avoid four quick heart losers.

TIP 90:

Part 1: Keep length with dummy.

When dummy has four cards in a suit and you also hold four cards, do not discard the suit if you could win a trick. If dummy holds five cards in a suit and you hold four or five cards, retain your length if you could win a trick.

(1)   A Q 6 4   (2)   K Q 7 6 4

   J 10 8   9 5 3 2   J 8   9 5 3 2

       K 7   A 10

(1) South has three winners. If East discards from this suit, dummy's last card becomes high and South makes four tricks.

(2) South has three winners and can set up a fourth trick if dummy has an entry. If East discards, declarer has five winners and does not need an outside entry to dummy.

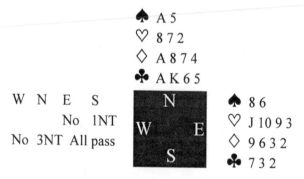

                 ♠ A 5
                 ♡ 8 7 2
                 ◇ A 8 7 4
                 ♣ A K 6 5

W N E S   ♠ 8 6

     No 1NT   ♡ J 10 9 3

No 3NT All pass   ◇ 9 6 3 2

                      ♣ 7 3 2

West leads the ♠K, ducked in dummy and continues with the ♠Q. A club to South's queen, is followed by the ♣J and a third club to dummy, West playing ♣10, ♣9, ♣4. What should East discard when the fourth club is played from dummy?

East should throw a heart and retain four diamonds, keeping length with dummy, otherwise declarer has nine tricks. South holds:

      ♠ 7 4 3   ♡ K Q 6 5   ◇ K Q 5   ♣ Q J 8

West has also shown heart strength with two signals. What are they?

At trick 2 West led the ♠Q, an unnecessarily high spade, since any spade would have been enough to dislodge the ♠A. The high card shows the entry in the high suit (spades excluded). Then, partner played the clubs in an abnormal order. Holding ♣10-9-4, the normal order would be 4 – 9 – 10. Partner played the highest one each time, sending a message that the entry is in the high suit, hearts.

Part 2: Keep length with declarer.

Just as it is vital to retain length in dummy's suit to prevent extra tricks, so it is imperative to retain length in a suit held by declarer.

	7 4		South has three tricks but if East
J 10 8		9 6 3 2	discards one, South will make
	A K Q 5		four tricks.

Keeping length with declarer is more difficult since declarer's hand is not visible but the bidding often reveals what declarer would rather keep hidden. Pay attention to the bidding and your discarding problems may be simplified.

North	South	Declarer has shown 4 hearts and 4 spades. A
	1NT	defender holding four hearts should be very
2♣	2♡	reluctant to part with one.
3NT	4♠	
No		

North	South	Declarer has denied a major and so will have
	1NT	4+ cards in a minor. If declarer shows up with
2♣	2♢	two or three cards in one minor, there must be
3NT	No	four or five cards in the other minor.

North	South	Declarer has shown 4 hearts and 5+ diamonds.
	1♢	A defender with length in diamonds should
1♠	2♡	keep that length.
4♡	No	

North	South	Having denied 4 hearts, 4 spades and 4 diamonds,
1♢	1NT	declarer should have 4+ clubs. Hang on to your
3NT	No	clubs with four or more.

TIP 91:

Make a mental note of declarer's likely shape during the bidding.

On many occasions the opponents will give away significant information about their holdings. Instead of wallowing in self-pity about the rotten hands you have been receiving, spend your time fruitfully by estimating declarer's likely hand pattern. Continue this assessment after dummy appears and many defensive opportunities can become crystal clear.

(1)

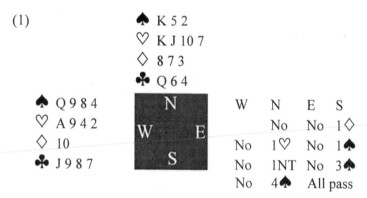

$\spadesuit$ K 5 2
$\heartsuit$ K J 10 7
$\diamondsuit$ 8 7 3
$\clubsuit$ Q 6 4

$\spadesuit$ Q 9 8 4
$\heartsuit$ A 9 4 2
$\diamondsuit$ 10
$\clubsuit$ J 9 8 7

W	N	E	S
		No	No	1$\diamondsuit$
No	1$\heartsuit$	No	1$\spadesuit$
No	1NT	No	3$\spadesuit$
No	4$\spadesuit$	All pass	

West leads the $\clubsuit$7: four, ten, ace. South continues with the $\heartsuit$8. Should West play the ace or play low to give declarer a guess?

(2)

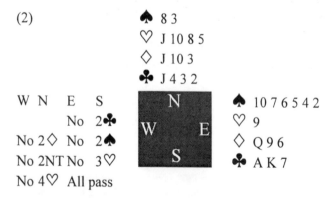

$\spadesuit$ 8 3
$\heartsuit$ J 10 8 5
$\diamondsuit$ J 10 3
$\clubsuit$ J 4 3 2

$\spadesuit$ 10 7 6 5 4 2
$\heartsuit$ 9
$\diamondsuit$ Q 9 6
$\clubsuit$ A K 7

W	N	E	S
		No	2$\clubsuit$
No	2$\diamondsuit$	No	2$\spadesuit$
No	2NT	No	3$\heartsuit$
No	4$\heartsuit$	All pass	

West leads the $\clubsuit$10. How should East plan the defence?

(1) South's bidding has revealed a 6-5 pattern, five spades as they were rebid and therefore 6+ diamonds since they were bid ahead of the spades. With a 5-5 pattern, the spades would have been bid first.

South's club at trick 1 accounts for twelve cards and therefore South's heart is a singleton. This is no time to play low smoothly as South has no guess in hearts. If you play low, the ♡K will be played and your ♡A will go begging. Grab the ♡A and play the ♣J next.

If South is no better than ♠ A J 7 6 3 ♡ 8 ◇ A Q J 9 5 4 ♣ A, you are well on the way to defeating the contract. If you duck, declarer can cope easily.

(2) After the artificial 2♣ : 2◇ beginning, South's 2♠ rebid promised 5+ spades. Add your six spades to dummy's doubleton and you can 'see' partner's spade void. Win with the ♣K (defenders win as cheaply as possible) and lead the ♠2 for partner to ruff. Regain the lead (hopefully) with the club ace and the next spade ruff will cook declarer's goose. South's hand:

♠ A K Q J 9 ♡ A K Q 7 6 ◇ A ♣ Q 5

Clearly you must not cash the second club before giving partner a spade ruff, otherwise you have no re-entry to give partner the second spade ruff, which is needed to beat the contract. Also, note the importance of winning trick 1 with the ♣K. West will thus know that you have the ♣A as well. If you win trick 1 with the ♣A, West will assume you do not have the ♣K. On ruffing the spade, West might play you for the ◇A and then declarer will make the contract.

TIP 92:

Make a mental note of declarer's likely point count during the bidding. As soon as dummy appears, count dummy's points.

Dummy's HCP are revealed after the opening lead. Add your HCP to dummy's and add opener's likely HCP range. Deduct this from 40 and partner's range of HCP becomes known. Often this will help you to calculate the defensive chances. For example, if partner's possible range is 4-6 points and partner has already turned up with an ace, it is futile to defend in the hope that partner might have an additional ace or king.

```
                  ♠ K Q 6 5
                  ♥ Q J 10 5
                  ◇ A 7
                  ♣ J 6 2
W   N   E   S                        ♠ 8
            1NT                      ♥ K 7 6 2
No 2♣  Dble2♥                        ◇ J 9 8
No 4♥  All pass                      ♣ A K Q 10 4
```

West leads the ♣8: two, ten, five. When you cash the next club, West plays the ♣7. How should East continue?

Without looking back at the problem, how many HCP are in dummy? If you do not have the answer at your fingertips, you are not using one of the best defensive clues. Dummy has 13 HCP, East began with 13 HCP and South with 12-14. That is a total of 38-40 HCP, which means partner's range is 0-2. Partner's ♣8-then-♣7 showed a doubleton so that you can cash another club, but to play the ♠8 after that would be foolish. Partner cannot have the ♠A.

Your best hope is that partner has the ♥8 or ♥9. Cash the third club and play a fourth club. If declarer's trumps are ♥A-9-4-3, partner's ♥8 can force dummy's ♥10 (it would not help South to ruff with the ♥9), and if you then cover either of dummy's remaining trump honours, you guarantee a trump trick to set the contract.

TIP 93:

Switch to lowest card = 'Please return this suit.' Switch to a high spot card = 'I have no interest in this suit.'

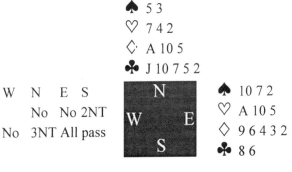

```
              ♠ 5 3
              ♡ 7 4 2
              ◇ A 10 5
              ♣ J 10 7 5 2
W   N   E   S        N          ♠ 10 7 2
    No  No  2NT   W      E      ♡ A 10 5
No  3NT All pass     S          ◇ 9 6 4 3 2
                                ♣ 8 6
```

West leads the ♠6 and East's ♠10 is taken by the ♠J. South leads the ♣K, which West wins with the ace. West switches to a heart and East is in with the ♡A. How should East continue?

The answer is that East does not know how to continue without considering the actual heart led. If West has switched to the ♡9, East should take the ♡A and return the ♠7 (top from the remaining doubleton). West will hold something like this:

♠ A Q 8 6 4   ♡ 9 8 6 3   ◇ 8 7   ♣ A 3

The spade return will defeat 3NT. West knows from East's ♠10 that South still has at least ♠K-9 left (see Tip 83). It is therefore vital to put East on lead for a spade through South. West chooses the *nine* of hearts as the switch in order to deny interest in a heart return.

If West has shifted to the ♡3, East should win with the ♡A and return the ♡10 (top of the remaining doubleton). West might have:

♠ Q 9 8 6 4   ♡ K J 9 3   ◇ 8 7   ♣ A 3

This time the heart return is essential to beat 3NT. With this spade holding, West knows after trick 1 that South holds ♠A-K-J and the spades cannot be established in time. West switches to the *three* of hearts, the lowest, to ask East to return a heart. East must co-operate, for a spade return would give declarer ten tricks.

TIP 94:

Clarify the defence for partner whenever possible.

On many occasions the path for the defence is clear to one partner but not to the other. The Basic Law of Partnership Bridge: 'If partner has a guess, partner will guess wrongly.' If you know how the defence should go, your duty is to leave partner in no doubt, if that is possible.

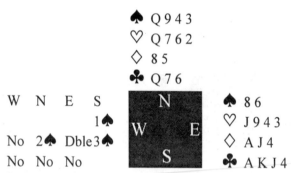

```
                  ♠ Q 9 4 3
                  ♡ Q 7 6 2
                  ◇ 8 5
                  ♣ Q 7 6
W    N    E    S         N        ♠ 8 6
               1♠                 ♡ J 9 4 3
No   2♣  Dble 3♠   W        E     ◇ A J 4
No   No   No              S       ♣ A K J 4
```

West leads the ◇K. What should East play on that? How should East plan the *defence*?

Recognising that the defence needs five tricks (Tip 81), East can see that there are only two diamond tricks for the defence and so three clubs may be needed. While the need for a club switch is clear to East, West may have no inkling that the source of extra tricks will be clubs. Suppose West has:

      ♠ 5 2   ♡ 8 5   ◇ K Q 10 9 3 2   ♣ 9 5 3

If East discourages diamonds with ◇4, or ◇4-◇J if West continues with the ◇Q, most Wests will switch to the ♡8. That will give South four heart tricks, as South has ♡A-K-10, and the contract.

South: ♠ A K J 10 7   ♡ A K 10   ◇ 7 6 ♣ 10 8 2

Rather than argue with West after the hand is over (remember, nobody wins a *post mortem*) East should overtake the ◇K with the ◇A, cash the ♣K (to show partner where the tricks are) and play the ◇4 to West for the club return and five tricks for the defence. Incidentally, a *post mortem* should seek to fix only the mistake, not the blame.

TIP 95:

Take control of the defence if you know what to do and partner may not be sure.

This is similar to Tip 94 except that here partner need not be involved in the defence because you know which suit must be attacked.

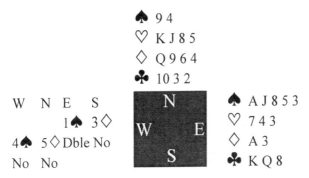

```
            ♠ 9 4
            ♡ K J 8 5
            ◇ Q 9 6 4
            ♣ 10 3 2

W  N  E  S      N         ♠ A J 8 5 3
      1♠ 3◇   W     E     ♡ 7 4 3
4♠ 5◇ Dble No             ◇ A 3
No No           S         ♣ K Q 8
```

The 3◇ jump-overcall showed 11-15 HCP and a decent 6+ suit. With a balanced hand, East naturally chooses to defend than to compete to the 5-level. West leads the ♠K. Plan East's defence.

Observing Tip 81, East notes that three tricks are needed. The likely tricks are one or two spades, one diamond and one club. If West has five spades, there will be no second spade trick. In that case it will be essential to score a club trick. East knows that while West does not. Therefore East must take control of the defence: overtake the ♠K and switch to the ♣K. This would be essential if South's hand is:

♠ 7   ♡ A Q 2   ◇ K J 10 8 7 5 2   ♣ A 7

Left on lead, West might continue spades or switch to hearts. Either is fatal for the defence. South wins and leads a trump. After drawing East's low trump, South discards the club loser on the hearts. If East wins trick 1 with the ♠A and switches to the ♣K, South will fail.

Corollary: If unsure how to continue, *do not take control of the defence.* For example, do not overtake partner's card if you do not know what to do next. If declarer leads towards low cards in dummy, do not play high to win the trick if you cannot tell how to continue to best effect.

TIP 96:

Beware of tipping declarer off about the nature of your hand
with your discards. The first discard chosen by most defenders is
from a 5-card or longer suit. Astute declarers often use that as
the basis for planning their play.

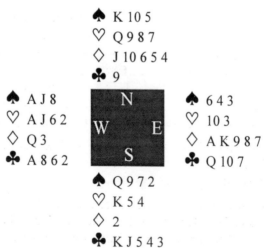

♠ A J 8
♡ A J 6 2
◇ Q 3
♣ A 8 6 2

♠ 6 4 3
♡ 10 3
◇ A K 9 8 7
♣ Q 10 7

West opened a strong 1NT and East bid 3NT. North led the ♡7,
three, king, ace. West played the ♣A, nine, seven, three, followed by
the ♣2 to the ten and jack, with North discarding ◇4. Back came the
♡5, two, queen, ten, and North returned the ♡8, ◇7 from dummy,
♡4 from South and West won with the ♡J.

Next came the ♣6, to the queen and king, North discarding ♠5, and
South exited with the ♠2. West won with the ♠A, as North
followed with the ♠10. How would you continue as West?

This was the complete deal:

♠ K 10 5
♡ Q 9 8 7
◇ J 10 6 5 4
♣ 9

♠ A J 8
♡ A J 6 2
◇ Q 3
♣ A 8 6 2

♠ 6 4 3
♡ 10 3
◇ A K 9 8 7
♣ Q 10 7

♠ Q 9 7 2
♡ K 5 4
◇ 2
♣ K J 5 4 3

There are a number of ways that the contract might have been beaten (North could ducked the second heart or South could switch to a low spade at trick 3) but in a 2002 Australian National Championship, the play went as described. This was the position after the first seven tricks:

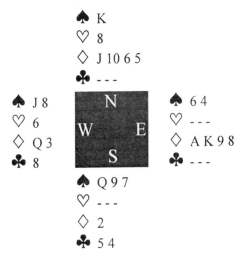

```
                    ♠ K
                    ♡ 8
                    ◇ J 10 6 5
                    ♣ - - -
    ♠ J 8                         ♠ 6 4
    ♡ 6                           ♡ - - -
    ◇ Q 3                         ◇ A K 9 8
    ♣ 8                           ♣ - - -
                    ♠ Q 9 7
                    ♡ - - -
                    ◇ 2
                    ♣ 5 4
```

Declarer, Australian international Bob Richman, had taken four tricks and had a club winner and three diamond tricks available. One extra trick was needed, but where could that be found?

Richman cashed the ♣8 and North had to let the ♠K go. Richman now pondered over the early ◇4 discard. Would North have thrown a deceptive ◇4 from ◇J-6-5-4-2 or ◇10-6-5-4-2? Reading the ◇4 to be the lowest of five because of that first discard, Richman placed North with ◇J-10-6-5-4. He led the ◇3, five, eight, two! He crossed to the ◇Q and exited with the ♡6. North won but had only diamonds left and became the stepping-stone for declarer to reach dummy.

It would not have helped North to insert a diamond honour. Dummy would win and a diamond to the queen and the ♡6 exit would again force North to give dummy the last two tricks.

Had North discarded a spade at trick 3 or a more deceptive ◇6, declarer might have been less inclined to take the chosen line. The moral: *Beware of telltale discards, especially against strong players.*

TIP 97:

Obey partner's signals.

The function of most signalling is to let partner know what to do. Except for mechanical count signals, which indicate the number of cards in a suit, signals usually indicate the direction the defence should take. A discouraging signal asks you not to continue the suit led. An encouraging signal requests you to keep on with the suit led. A suit-preference signal indicates the suit you wish partner to play.

If partner gives you an attitude or a suit-preference signal, you need justification 'beyond reasonable doubt' to act contrary to partner's signal. Even if partner's request seems abnormal, trust a competent partner, not the opposition.

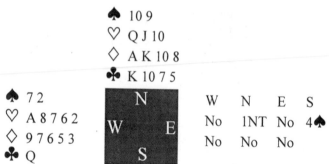

```
              ♠  10 9
              ♡  Q J 10
              ◇  A K 10 8
              ♣  K 10 7 5
 ♠ 7 2          N           W    N    E    S
 ♡ A 8 7 6 2                No  1NT  No  4♠
 ◇ 9 7 6 5 3    W    E      No   No  No
 ♣ Q            S
```

West leads the ♣Q: king, ace, ♣4 from declarer. East returns the ♣2, ruffed by West. How should West continue?

East has requested a diamond switch with the *two* of clubs (lowest card asks for the lowest suit back when giving a ruff or hoping that partner will ruff). A diamond switch seems foolish in view of dummy's strength and if partner has never heard of a suit-preference signal, you may look elsewhere (preferably for a better partner).

Ignore the diamond request at your peril if partner is competent and attentive. You would be very sorry if you try to cash the ♡A first and it turns out that South holds:

    ♠ A K Q 8 5 4   ♡ - - -   ◇ Q J 4 2 ♣ J 8 4

TIP 98:

Watch partner's spot cards for secondary signals.

Spare cards can be used to give a suit-preference signal. If you have played the 2 as a count signal from 9-5-2, you can play the 5 or 9 next. Normal order is 2-5-9. If you depart from the normal order, you are giving a suit-preference signal (See Tip 88). The 9 on the second round would be a request for the higher outside suit. Playing the 5 would show no preference at all or preference for the lower suit.

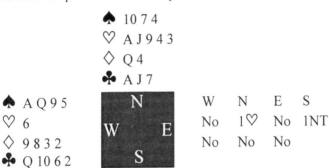

```
              ♠ 10 7 4
              ♡ A J 9 4 3
              ◊ Q 4
              ♣ A J 7
 ♠ A Q 9 5        N        W    N    E    S
 ♡ 6                       No   1♡   No   1NT
 ◊ 9 8 3 2    W       E    No   No   No
 ♣ Q 10 6 2       S
```

West leads the ♣2: seven, king, five. East returns the ♣8: nine, queen, ace. (Note: The unnecessary play of the ♣Q can be taken as a suit-preference request for spades). The play continues:

3. ◊Q from dummy: king, ace, eight
4. ♡5 from declarer: six, nine, queen
5. ♣4 from East: three, six, jack
6. ♡3 from dummy: king, seven, and you discard a diamond
7. ♠2 from East : six , queen, four
8. West cashes the ♣10: ♠7 dummy, ♡8 from East, ◊5 from South.

How should West continue?

East's ♡8 is significant. The bidding and play mark South with ♡10-7-5 and East with ♡K-Q-8-2. East's ♡8 discard from ♡8-2 asks West to play the higher suit. Play the ♠A next and take 1NT two down. If you exit 'safely' with a diamond, declarer will succeed. The South hand: ♠ K 6   ♡ 10 7 5   ◊ A J 7 6 5   ♣ J 8 4

TIP 99:

The queen-signal by partner under your ace or king lead is either a singleton or guarantees the jack.

Discarding an honour promises the honour below and denies the honour above. A discard of an ace promises the king-queen. Discarding a king shows the queen-jack and discarding a queen shows the jack-ten. The queen signal on partner's ace or king lead has a similar function By confirming the jack or a singleton queen, it tells partner that it is safe to lead low next. You guarantee that you will win the trick. It follows that you must not drop the queen from queen-doubleton unless it is Q-J doubleton.

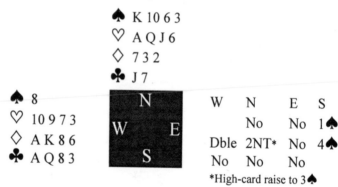

		♠ K 10 6 3			
		♡ A Q J 6			
		◇ 7 3 2			
		♣ J 7			

♠ 8			W	N	E	S
♡ 10 9 7 3				No	No	1♠
◇ A K 8 6			Dble	2NT*	No	4♠
♣ A Q 8 3			No	No	No	

*High-card raise to 3♠

West leads the ◇A and East plays the ◇Q. How should West proceed?

West wants to have East on lead to bring a club through declarer into West's ♣A-Q. The missing hands could be:

East: ♠ 7 4   ♡ 5 4 2   ◇ Q J 10 4   ♣ 9 5 4 2

South: ♠ A Q J 9 5 2   ♡ K 8   ◇ 9 5   ♣ K 10 6

When West continues with the ◇6 at trick 2, East wins and has no trouble finding the club switch to take the contract down. If West had started ◇A, ◇K, declarer will make 4♠ by discarding two clubs on the hearts after trumps have been drawn. If East does not play the ◇Q at trick 1, West has a tough time finding the low diamond next.

142

On this deal, cover the East and South cards and plan West's defence after the given auction and play to trick 1:

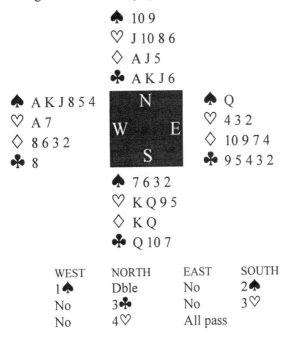

```
              ♠ 10 9
              ♡ J 10 8 6
              ◇ A J 5
              ♣ A K J 6
♠ A K J 8 5 4      N        ♠ Q
♡ A 7          W       E    ♡ 4 3 2
◇ 8 6 3 2                   ◇ 10 9 7 4
♣ 8                S        ♣ 9 5 4 3 2
              ♠ 7 6 3 2
              ♡ K Q 9 5
              ◇ K Q
              ♣ Q 10 7
```

WEST	NORTH	EAST	SOUTH
1♠	Dble	No	2♠
No	3♣	No	3♡
No	4♡	All pass	

West leads the ♠A and East follows with the ♠Q. South the ♠2. How should West continue?

Applying Tip 81, West can count two spade tricks and the ♡A. How will a fourth trick materialise? Partner's queen signal here has to be a singleton as West holds the ♠J. Thus, partner can ruff a spade.

Should West play ♠K and a third spade, hoping East can over-ruff dummy? Not likely. As South's 2♠ reply showed game-going strength, South should hold almost all of the 12 HCP missing.

There is a better plan. West should switch to the ♣8, take the ♡A on the first round of trumps and then lead the ♠4 (lowest card for the low suit return) for East to ruff. When East plays a club back, West's ruff beats the contract.

TIP 100:

Part 1: Red on red, black on black

We are all prone to human failings and a good defender can exploit weaknesses. One method is to prey on a lapse of concentration when declarer is drawing trumps or tackling a long suit. If you are out of the suit declarer is leading, play a card of the same colour. If hearts are trumps, 'follow' with a diamond; if declarer is playing spades, try discarding a club. If not sufficiently alert, declarer may miscount the suit.

Use red-on-red or black-on-black only when you have no important signal to send and can spare a card in the suit of the same colour. It will rarely work against an expert or early in a session, but after three hours of play, many a player's mental energy has been known to wilt. Seeing a card of the same colour, it is easy to assume that a player has followed suit. How often have you heard a declarer say, 'I thought all the trumps had gone', possibly another victim of red-on-red, black-on-black?

Part 2: Red on black, black on red

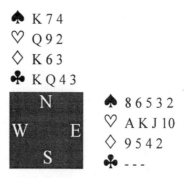

♠ K 7 4
♡ Q 9 2
◇ K 6 3
♣ K Q 4 3

♠ 8 6 5 3 2
♡ A K J 10
◇ 9 5 4 2
♣ - - -

After 1NT : 3NT, West leads the ♣5. What should East discard? Playing standard signals East plans to throw the ♠2 and the ◇2 to discourage those suits and suggest a heart switch. Discard the ◇2 first, red on black. Play a card of the opposite colour when you want to wake partner up that you are not following suit. Partner should not need such a jolt, but we all know what partners are really like, don't we?

Happy bridging.